THE GREEK TRAGEDY
IN NEW TRANSLATIONS

GENERAL EDITORS
Peter Burian and Alan Shapiro

SOPHOCLES: Oedipus at Colonus

SOPHOCLES

Oedipus at Colonus

Translated by
EAMON GRENNAN
and
RACHEL KITZINGER

OXFORD
UNIVERSITY PRESS

2005

OXFORD
UNIVERSITY PRESS

Oxford   New York
Auckland   Bangkok   Buenos Aires   Cape Town   Chennai
Dar es Salaam   Delhi   Hong Kong   Istanbul   Karachi   Kolkata
Kuala Lumpur   Madrid   Melbourne   Mexico City   Mumbai
Nairobi   São Paulo   Shanghai   Taipei   Tokyo   Toronto

Copyright © 2005 by Oxford University Press, Inc.

Published by Oxford University Press, Inc.
198 Madison Avenue, New York, NY 10016
www.oup.com

Oxford is a registered trademark of Oxford University Press

Library of Congress Cataloging-in-Publication Data
Sophocles.
[Oedipus at Colonus. English]
Oedipus at Colonus / Sophocles ; translated by Eamon Grennan
and Rachel Kitzinger.
p.   cm.—(The Greek tragedy in new translations)
Includes bibliographical references.
ISBN-13: 978-0-19-513504-0
ISBN-10: 0-19-513504-0
1. Oedipus (Greek mythology)—Drama.
I. Grennan, Eamon, 1941–   II. Kitzinger, Rachel, 1948–
III. Title.   IV. Series.
PA4414.O5G74   2004
882'.01—dc22
2004046500

9 8 7 6 5 4 3 2 1
Printed in the United States of America

To the memory of Ernst Kitzinger (1912–2003)
and for our daughter, Kira.

EDITORS' FOREWORD

"*The Greek Tragedy in New Translations* is based on the conviction that poets like Aeschylus, Sophocles, and Euripides can only be properly rendered by translators who are themselves poets. Scholars may, it is true, produce useful and perceptive versions. But our most urgent present need is for a *re-creation* of these plays—as though they had been written, freshly and greatly, by masters fully at home in the English of our own times."

With these words, the late William Arrowsmith announced the purpose of this series, and we intend to honor that purpose. As was true of most of the volumes that began to appear in the 1970s—first under Arrowsmith's editorship, later in association with Herbert Golder—those for which we bear editorial responsibility are products of close collaboration between poets and scholars. We believe (as Arrowsmith did) that the skills of both are required for the difficult and delicate task of transplanting these magnificent specimens of another culture into the soil of our own place and time, to do justice both to their deep differences from our patterns of thought and expression and to their palpable closeness to our most intimate concerns. Above all, we are eager to offer contemporary readers dramatic poems that convey as vividly and directly as possible the splendor of language, the complexity of image and idea, and the intensity of emotion of the originals. This entails, among much else, the recognition that the tragedies were meant for performance—as scripts for actors—to be sung and danced as well as spoken. It demands writing of inventiveness, clarity, musicality, and dramatic power. By such standards we ask that these translations be judged.

This series is also distinguished by its recognition of the need of nonspecialist readers for a critical introduction informed by the best recent scholarship, but written clearly and without condescension.

Each play is followed by notes designed not only to elucidate obscure references but also to mediate the conventions of the Athenian stage as well as those features of the Greek text that might otherwise go unnoticed. The notes are supplemented by a glossary of mythical and geographical terms that should make it possible to read the play without turning elsewhere for basic information. Stage directions are sufficiently ample to aid readers in imagining the action as they read. Our fondest hope, of course, is that these versions will be staged not only in the minds of their readers but also in the theaters to which, after so many centuries, they still belong.

A NOTE ON THE SERIES FORMAT

A series such as this requires a consistent format. Different translators, with individual voices and approaches to the material in hand, cannot be expected to develop a single coherent style for each of the three tragedians, much less make clear to modern readers that, despite the differences among the tragedians themselves, the plays share many conventions and a generic, or period, style. But they can at least share a common format and provide similar forms of guidance to the reader.

1. *Spelling of Greek names*

Orthography is one area of difference among the translations that requires a brief explanation. Historically, it has been common practice to use Latinized forms of Greek names when bringing them into English. Thus, for example, Oedipus (not Oidipous) and Clytemnestra (not Klutaimestra) are customary in English. Recently, however, many translators have moved toward more precise transliteration, which has the advantage of presenting the names as both Greek and new, instead of Roman and neoclassical importations into English. In the case of so familiar a name as Oedipus, however, transliteration risks the appearance of pedantry or affectation. And in any case, perfect consistency cannot be expected in such matters. Readers will feel the same discomfort with "Athenai" as the chief city of Greece as they would with "Platon" as the author of the *Republic*.

The earlier volumes in this series adopted as a rule a "mixed" orthography in accordance with the considerations outlined above. The most familiar names retain their Latinate forms, the rest are transliterated; *–os* rather than Latin *–us* is adopted for the termination of masculine names, and Greek diphthongs (such as Iphige*neia* for Latin Iphigenia) are retained. Some of the later volumes continue this practice, but where translators have preferred to use a more consistent practice of transliteration or Latinization, we have honored their wishes.

2. *Stage directions*

The ancient manuscripts of the Greek plays do not supply stage directions (though the ancient commentators often provide information relevant to staging, delivery, "blocking," etc.). Hence stage directions must
be inferred from words and situations and our knowledge of Greek
theatrical conventions. At best this is a ticklish and uncertain proce-
dure. But it is surely preferable that good stage directions should be
provided by the translator than that readers should be left to their own
devices in visualizing action, gesture, and spectacle. Ancient tragedy
was austere and "distanced" by means of masks, which means that the
reader must not expect the detailed intimacy ("He shrugs and turns
wearily away," "She speaks with deliberate slowness, as though to em-
phasize the point," etc.) that characterizes stage directions in modern
naturalistic drama.

3. *Numbering of lines*

For the convenience of the reader who may wish to check the translation against the original, or vice versa, the lines have been numbered
according to both the Greek and English texts. The lines of the translation have been numbered in multiples of ten, and those numbers
have been set in the right-hand margin. The (inclusive) Greek nu-
meration will be found bracketed at the top of the page. The Notes
that follow the text have been keyed to both numerations, the line
numbers of the translation in **bold**, followed by the Greek line numbers in regular type, and the same convention is used for all references
to specific passages (of the translated plays only) in both the Notes and
the Introduction.

Readers will doubtless note that in many plays the English lines
outnumber the Greek, but they should not therefore conclude that the
translator has been unduly prolix. In some cases the reason is simply
that the translator has adopted the free-flowing norms of modern Anglo-
American prosody, with its brief-breath-and emphasis-determined lines,
and its habit of indicating cadence and caesuras by line length and
setting rather than by conventional punctuation. Even where translators
have preferred to cast dialogue in more regular five-beat or six-beat
lines, the greater compactness of Greek diction is likely to result in a
substantial disparity in Greek and English numerations.

Durham, N.C.   PETER BURIAN
Chapel Hill, N.C.   ALAN SHAPIRO

CONTENTS

OEDIPUS AT COLONUS

INTRODUCTION

The *Oedipus at Colonus*, written by Sophocles in the last years of his life (he died in 406 BCE) and not produced until after his death (perhaps in 401 BCE), is a powerful exploration of what survives endings—the ending of an individual life (Oedipus dies at the end of the play); the ending of a city (in 404 Sophocles' native city, Athens, came to the end of its role as the primary political presence in the Mediterranean world through its defeat by Sparta and its allies after a long and costly war); and the end of the poet's own life (Sophocles was probably ninety when he wrote the play). The play is composed out of this sense of familiar and known things coming to an end, as it looks back at the figure of Oedipus as a young man and at Sophocles' treatment of his story in his earlier plays, *Antigone* (442?) and *Oedipus Tyrannus* (430?). But the play also looks forward to a future that Sophocles offers his play as a way of facing and even welcoming—however unknowable and strange that future might be.

THE TWO EARLIER PLAYS

By 406 BCE Sophocles had written about 125 plays—tragedies and satyr plays—to be performed at the City Dionysia, the annual civic celebration in Athens of the god Dionysus. Seven of these 125 plays have survived, and three of these seven center on the myth of Oedipus. In 442?, Sophocles wrote the *Antigone*, whose story comes at the end of the myth of the Labdacids, the family of Laius and his son, Oedipus. Oedipus' male children (and brothers), Eteocles and Polyneices, are engaged in a dispute over succession to the kingship of Thebes. Polyneices makes an alliance with neighboring Argos and brings an army to attack Thebes. In the course of the battle the brothers kill each other, fulfilling their father/brother's curse on them. The *Antigone* begins on the day after the battle when Creon, the boys' uncle, has decreed that one, Eteocles, is to be buried with full honor, as he died defending Thebes, while Polyneices' corpse is to be left to rot, as Creon considers him a traitor to Thebes. Their sister, Antigone, refuses to acknowledge the political distinction between the brothers, buries Polyneices, and is condemned to death by Creon. Rather than waiting to die in the tomb in which Creon has buried her alive, Antigone kills herself, thus essentially ending the line of Oedipus and the story of Oedipus' tragic marriage to his mother, Jocasta (although Ismene, Oedipus' other daughter, survives, her story ends with Antigone's death).

Ten years later Sophocles writes the *Oedipus Tyrannus*, which dramatizes Oedipus' own discovery of the fact of that marriage and his earlier murder of his father, Laius. The setting of this play is again the unfortunate Thebes, this time being devastated by a plague. Oedipus, as Thebes' king, is determined to save the city and its inhabitants from this destruction. As he relentlessly follows the clues the god Apollo has given him about the cause of the plague, he uncovers the story of his own past: his chance meeting with his (unknown) father whom he kills in a dispute over a right of way, and his marriage to his (unknown) mother, Jocasta, as a result of his inspired answer to the Sphinx's riddle. Marriage to Jocasta was his reward from a grateful Thebes, which had been devastated by the attacks of the Sphinx. She could be stopped only by an answer to her riddle, "What walks on four legs in the morning, two legs at noon, and three legs in the evening and has a single voice?" Oedipus' answer—"man"—he will spend the rest of his life coming to understand. The reward the Cadmeians (another name for the Thebans) offer him for ridding them of the Sphinx is the throne of Thebes and marriage to the queen, Jocasta, Oedipus' mother. As Oedipus relentlessly pursues the truth about this past, Jocasta is the first to understand what has happened, and, anticipating her failure to stop Oedipus from discovering and revealing the whole story, she hangs herself. When Oedipus finally reconstructs the story and recognizes that he is both the destroyer and the savior of Thebes, he fulfills the curse he himself has placed on the person responsible for the plague by blinding himself—in essence exiling himself from human society. The play ends with his unsuccessful attempt to persuade Jocasta's brother Creon, who has become king in his place, to complete the exile by banishing him from Thebes.

In these two plays we see the richness of this story for Sophocles' exploration of what tragedy as a genre can offer its audience. Against the backdrop of an extreme threat to a city's well-being, individuals struggle with each other and themselves to understand the limits of human action and understanding in the light of the patterns of an order outside their control. Neither play offers answers. Rather, both dramatize, in radically different ways, the dynamic struggle to make sense of the world through the choices humans make, the values they uphold by those choices, the limits of language to articulate and to persuade others of the correctness of those choices, and the irresolvable conflicts that ensue. The structure of the plot in each play arises out of the tension created by the power and futility of human attempts, through language and action, to construct a meaningful world. In the *Antigone*, the conflict between Antigone's and Creon's understandings of what the death of Polyneices and Eteocles demands of them, and how to fulfill those demands, is viscerally represented in the pushing of each side to destructive extremes, out of which a restorative compromise can be imagined only as the product of extreme suffering. The action of the play is structured around a series of confrontations between two characters in which the opposition, which seems absolute and fixed, in fact moves Antigone and Creon, the two main opponents, to see the destructive results of their passionately held positions. In the *Oedipus Tyrannus* Oedipus' driving determination to keep asking questions gives the play a powerful sense of precipitous linear movement, which, as it takes the audience into the future, in fact takes us back into the past, until the two come together at the brink of a chasm of despair from which it is hard to imagine the possibility of recovery.

THE STRUCTURE OF THE *OEDIPUS AT COLONUS*

The structure of the *Oedipus at Colonus* is quite different. It moves forward neither by opposition nor by a driving, if complex, linear motion. Rather, the *Oedipus at Colonus* moves in waves of arrivals and departures in counterpoint with the single arc of Oedipus' faltering arrival at the beginning of the play, his seated presence at center stage throughout the action until the very end, and his dramatic departure at the end, without assistance and accompanied by lightning, thunder, and the voice of a god. At issue in these waves of coming and going are the laws, the patterns—in Greek, the *nomoi* (a word that means both law, custom, and melody)—by which we order our lives, in conjunction with a pattern we cannot know but which provides a kind of counterpoint, constantly transforming the meaning we think we are creating. Oedipus serves as the focal point of this conjunction, and in the paradoxes and judgments that arise from his presence the audience catches a glimpse of the ineffable harmony between what changes and what remains unchanging—between the human and divine, the knowable and the unknowable, the powerless and the powerful.

For the audience at the end of the fifth century this play is

Sophocles' gift to the city-state in which he had lived and which he had served his entire life. Athens' attempt at a new form of government, democracy, seemed to be reaching a crisis in its final defeat by the oligarchic Spartans, with whom Athens had been at war, on and off, for twenty-five years. In this play the death of Oedipus in Colonus, Sophocles' own birthplace and a town within sight of the Acropolis, promises to the Athenians the protection of the hero forever, some kind of eternal life for the city. The city's survival is perhaps not to be imagined as the preservation of the laws that have ordered its existence or the continuity of its political hegemony but as the manifestation of a spirit that the play only suggests, adumbrates like a mystery, in the complex interplay of the rhythms of its plot.

In the opening scene two figures enter the theater: an old, blind man and a young woman. They are travelers, beggars without home or possessions, and their arrival in this place, as in every place they come to, poses the question: How will they find what they need to survive? Stripped of everything that defines a life, what does their existence mean? Oedipus' opening speech begins to explain the sense he has made of this stage of his life, one so different from the complex layers of his earlier history, as Sophocles portrays it in the *Oedipus Tyrannus*, where everything turned out to mean more than it seemed, and all understanding led only to more mystery. He says of himself: "who asks little and gets less, though even less / than little is enough—" (5–6/5–6). He goes on to explain the things that allow him to be content, to be at peace with this bare existence ". . . the long / companionship of time, and bitter trouble, / and beyond that the manner I was born to, teach me / to be easy with whatever happens" (6–9/7–8). While these things allow him inner ease, he explains in the last lines of the speech the means by which he interacts with others to get what he needs: "As strangers / we've learned how to listen to the natives of a place / and to act according to what we hear" (13–15/12–13). He has learned an openness to the laws and habits of the particular place he comes to and a willingness to comply with the circumstances of the moment. This opening speech gives us the world of the play, the backdrop against which all that will happen is to be understood. Oedipus has defined the rhythms that finally, after years of struggle, allow him to live in some kind of difficult but resolved accommodation to the world and his own history. It is a life stripped to its essentials: the character one is born with, the accumulated experience of acting and suffering, the rhythm of change that time brings and an openness to whatever happens.

Against this backdrop is played out a series of encounters between

Oedipus and others, where others' actions, ambitions, and desires—their ways of being in the world—are tested and judged by the touchstone of Oedipus' achieved wisdom. In this way Oedipus turns out to be once again, as he was in the *Oedipus Tyrannus*, a riddle: the combination of his apparent destitution and his enormous hidden power serves as a test of others' humanity, as each newcomer responds to the presence of the old, blind beggar seated on a bare rock. The Greeks understood all suppliants, as Oedipus is, as a test: those who are in need of protection challenge those with power to take the correct measure of their power as provisional and limited. It is out of an understanding that any human, however secure, could easily become as helpless as the suppliant and that all human power pales in comparison with the divine and eternal power of the gods, and especially of Zeus, who protects suppliants, that one is moved to put oneself at risk in the service of those who are powerless. But Oedipus is a different kind of test because he is, in fact, not helpless, although he seems to be, and in this way the *Oedipus at Colonus* is not merely a "suppliant play." His interactions are based not on a vivid disparity of power between himself and others, but rather on others' ability to understand the discrepancy between his appearance and the power he embodies, the discontinuity between his past and his future, the coexistence of his dependence and autonomy.

Oedipus' power comes not only from the understanding he has struggled to achieve. The first indication that the pattern of Oedipus' life is also shaped by something beyond his own understanding and the laws and customs of those he encounters comes in the second half of the opening scene, when Oedipus learns from an unnamed citizen of Colonus that he has taken a seat in the grove of the dread goddesses (Furies, Erinyes, Eumenides—they have many names and yet often go unnamed, just referred to as the Dread Ones). For the citizen of Colonus his presence there is a violation: the Eumenides are divinities so powerful that one must not even speak out loud in the vicinity of their sacred grove, much less walk into it and sit down. They are ancient earth goddesses whose role is to bring punishment to humans who commit the most basic and intense of crimes: violation of the natural, unalienable bonds between members of a family, the very basis of our common humanity. They are fierce and implacable—accepting no excuse, no explanation to moderate their punishment of violations in their sphere. For Oedipus, this grove is the place that he has known, from Apollo's prediction, would be the end of his journey, the place where finally he can rest. Here again is the riddle, now not on the level of human interactions with Oedipus but on the level of the rhythms and patterns outside human control that order the world: why would Oedipus, the greatest violator of family ties that we can imagine, find peace at last in the grove of the Eumenides?

What about Oedipus can make sense of this disparity between his past and his destined future? We learn later, from Ismene his daughter, who is the first visitor to approach Oedipus, that there is even more to this riddle. For Apollo has now prophesied that wherever Oedipus dies will be a source of eternal protection for the surrounding country, for whoever has accepted him and not asked him to move on. Here again the riddle: why is the polluted Oedipus to become a source of protection and safety for those willing to embrace him? And—looking beyond the ending of the play—what kind of protection does he offer, since his burial place in Colonus—the "bulwark" at the outskirts of Athens—has not kept the Athens of 402 BCE (when the play is first being performed, after Sophocles' death in 406) from devastating defeat at the hands of the Spartans? How then is the audience to understand the power that, in alliance with the divine world, Oedipus offers, which is so incongruent with his past story, his present state, and the imminent future of the audience watching the play?

The substance of these riddles plays out in two interweaving strands of action in the play. One corresponds to the riddle of the larger order: the transformation of Oedipus from helpless and blind old man when he first enters the stage to guide and authority at the end of the play, one whose place of death will have power after his death, as the object of a hero cult. This transformation is the mirror of, and answer to, the change that Oedipus undergoes from king to polluted being in the *Oedipus Tyrannus*, but now Oedipus is a knowing participant, in harmony with the rhythm of the transformation, which he knows will happen in its own time. The other strand is played out in the interaction between Oedipus and all those who come into contact with him, as he sits on his rock in the middle of the stage. Through these encounters, unfolding in the uncertain immediacy of the moment, what becomes possible is an understanding of a human order that can take account of Oedipus' paradoxical power. For example, the citizen of Colonus, who approaches Oedipus and Antigone as soon as they have settled in the grove, is the first to be tested by his presence. His response to the violation of the grove shows the kind of order he lives by. Despite all appearance he understands he must consult with all the citizens of Colonus before deciding what to do with Oedipus: "Stay there, / there where you first appeared, while I / go to the citizens (who live *here*, not in the city) / and tell them what's happened. For they will decide / to take you in or send you away" (89–93/77–80). This citizen, despite his knowledge of the inviolability of the grove, knows the appropriate rhythm of judgment he must demonstrate in response to Oedipus' intrusion: as a citizen, he cannot act without the rest of the citizen body—no matter how obvious it is that Oedipus is where he should not be.

THE CHORUS

When that body of citizens arrive, in the form of the chorus, they can claim with appropriate authority that Oedipus must move in order for them to talk to him, and Oedipus, on the basis of his openness to what is taught to him by the inhabitants of whatever place he comes to, can put in abeyance the knowledge that he belongs in the grove, to comply with their demand. Here, too, the different rhythms are in harmony, with Oedipus moving between his own understanding and that of the chorus, but Sophocles dramatizes vividly the difficulty in that harmony by the excruciating slowness and effort with which Oedipus moves from the rock where he has placed himself within the grove to the rock at its edge, where the chorus has insisted he sit to speak with them. It is only when, at their insistence, Oedipus reveals his identity that he becomes a test for the chorus; having accepted the anonymous beggar as a suppliant, they now want to drive Oedipus away.

The chorus is not, in Sophoclean tragedy, responsible for developing the action of the play, but rather reflects on that action from their perspective, as interpreters through the particular medium of song and dance of what they see. From their perspective, the story they have always heard of Oedipus' past makes his presence among them intolerable. Oedipus responds on their level, on the level of story and reputation, to question the validity of Athens' reputation as a city that accepts strangers, if the chorus demands that he leave:

> Then what's become of reputation? What good is
> a good name if it fades like morning dew?
> What good is it if Athens stands alone, as they say,
> a god-fearing city—alone able to save
> the sick, afflicted stranger. Where is the good in this for me,
> seeing—since my name alone makes you tremble—
> you'll drag me from this sanctuary here
> and drive me away? (275–82/258–65)

Because of Oedipus' challenge to the chorus to live up to the way their city is spoken of, to be consistent with the laws and customs it is known for, the chorus agrees to summon Theseus—the legendary king of Athens—to make a decision about Oedipus. As the figure whose action will represent Athens, what he does will reveal how Athenian law can, through actions based on the judgments it allows, respond to the riddle of Oedipus.

But the chorus throughout the play articulates another level of order, one that is abstracted from the mechanics of decision and action and creates in song and dance a kind of understanding that mediates between the human and divine worlds. As a body, the chorus, though characterized as older citizens of Colonus, is separated from the actors not only by performing exclusively in the orchestra, the circular area between the stage and the seats of the audience, but also by their form of expression: dance and choral song. While the chorus leader interacts with the characters in speech, when the chorus performs as a whole it is always in the form of sung lyrics and movement that follows the rhythm of the song. Their mode of expression and their language, in both form and content, remove the play's events from the contingency of the moment. This way of responding to Oedipus is first illustrated in the instructions that the chorus leader gives Oedipus so that he can perform a ritual of purification for his violation of the grove. In his detailed account of each step in the ritual, the chorus leader describes a series of actions abstracted from human choice, feeling, and even understanding, but nonetheless meaningful in relation to the divine power of the Eumenides and Oedipus' violation, as the chorus understands it, of their grove.

In their next four songs, when they lead Oedipus to tell the story of his past, or sing a hymn to Athens that represents the city in terms of its gods, their gifts to the city, and its natural beauty, or describe the battle between Theseus and Creon over the possession of Antigone and Ismene as a battle of right against wrong, or describe the misery that Oedipus' life represents as a headland beaten by waves from every direction, the chorus transforms the ever-changing, continuous struggle of human action into language whose rhythms, sound, and descriptive power create an ordered, self-contained poetic narrative with a formal integrity that is the closest humans can come to an expression of a permanent order. This, then, is the way the chorus responds to the challenge of Oedipus' presence. They leave the decision of what to do to Theseus, but they incorporate Oedipus' story and Athens' story into an order of their own, in the rhythms and movement of their song and dance. Within the context of the action and the choices the other characters are engaged in, the limit of the chorus's order is apparent in their restriction to the space of the orchestra and the movements of dance. But what they express in their dance and song is an essential dimension of the way humans make sense of their world.

EPISODES

In between the chorus's songs, the episodes dramatize the arrival of four visitors, each in his or her own way drawn to respond to Oedipus' presence in Athens. Very roughly, they fall into categories of friends and enemies. Ismene and Theseus give Oedipus what he needs to survive out of genuine feeling for him and a deep understanding of what the laws they live by demand of them. Polyneices and Creon come to gain control of Oedipus' power for their own ends, although they present themselves as acting out of pity for Oedipus' suffering and in his interest and argue on the basis of positive norms of behavior. In each case Oedipus both interprets and judges these characters' actions, culminating in the violent curse he places on his son—a curse that poses the deepest challenge to the audience's understanding of Oedipus' judgment. As we watch each encounter, we see the complexity of each character's response to Oedipus, in the incongruity between the way the laws of society order their behavior and the way that Oedipus, from the perspective he describes in the prologue, responds to them. This series of comings and goings, all centered on the question of where Oedipus belongs, creates a kind of dramatic fugue that plays out the various rhythms by which we live, rhythms created by the interplay of feeling, understanding, experience, and values.

At the center of these visitations is Creon's forceful removal of Antigone and Ismene and Theseus' return of them. This self-contained and unique action at the heart of the play has no apparent consequence: they are taken and returned within the course of two hundred lines or so, and there is no lasting effect of their departure. But it is another manifestation of the rhythms of loss and gain, strength and impotence, departure and return, violation and restoration, which represent Sophocles' understanding of what human experience must be. The rhythm of loss and restoration that Creon's abduction of the two women dramatizes mirrors on the level of human action the mysterious and divinely orchestrated transformation of Oedipus, from his entrance as a wandering beggar at the beginning of the play to his departure "home," summoned by a god, at the end.

In the first episode Ismene arrives to tell Oedipus of the oracles that make explicit the nature of the gift he offers to those who take him in and to bring him news of his two sons' struggle for the throne of Thebes. Her traveling alone through the countryside to find Oedipus is an absolute violation of the behavior appropriate to an unmarried woman, as is Antigone's wandering, which the care of her father requires. In fact, when Creon comes, he throws in Oedipus' face the debasement of the two women in the eyes of the world as an argument for Oedipus' return to Thebes. But Oedipus' judgment of his daughters and of his sons reveals the difficulty of basing one's choice of how to behave on social norms. He addresses his daughters about his sons:

> Ach, those two! In their nature, in their way of life,
> they mimic Egyptian habits. For the men of Egypt
> sit indoors weaving, while their wives
> go out every day in the world
> to provide what they need. So here you both are,
> while those fit for the task do housework
> like maids. The two of you do their work, this hard work—
> caring for my suffering self. (370–77/337–45)

Oedipus here claims that his children's behavior is uniquely counter to Greek social norms by evoking the "counter culture" of Egypt, which the Greeks viewed as a mirror image of their own society. By so doing he exposes the provisional nature of a judgment based solely on social norms, since in Egypt the children's behavior would be normal. Oedipus' comparison raises a further complication: from another perspective Antigone and Ismene are doing exactly what is expected of Greek women, caring for their male relation, while Eteocles and Polyneices are pursuing their political ambitions, exactly what would be expected of them as Greek men. By this comparison Oedipus wishes to condemn his sons for "staying at home" and pursuing their own interests and to praise his daughters for their courage in wandering the world to take care of him. If we understand his words simply on the level of social norms they fail to achieve his purpose, as they equate his sons and his daughters in the violation of those norms, and they also point to the ways in which his children are, in fact, meeting, not violating, expectations of behavior. It is clear, then, that when Oedipus uses Egypt to point to the "alien" behavior of his children, he is judging them not on the basis of a social order, the standards of which are relative and ambiguous, but on the basis of values that he does not or cannot at this point articulate but that become clear by the end of the play.

A similar complexity is involved in trying to understand and judge Theseus' and Creon's interactions with Oedipus. The two men can, from one perspective, be seen as examples of good and bad men in positions of power. Theseus' unquestioning acceptance of Oedipus and his offer of protection and a home amply fulfill Athens' reputation as an open society, able to find a place for whoever comes there. His controlled handling of Creon's abduction of Antigone and Ismene attest to his diplomacy and careful use of force, especially in contrast to Creon's provocative rhetoric and rash violence. Yet Theseus, by accepting Oedipus into Athens, establishes Thebes as a future enemy, a chilling reminder, for the audience of the play, of the war that has ended in Athenian defeat. And Creon, who is, on the surface, a shameless seeker after his own advantage, is acting on behalf of his city and at their request to bring Oedipus back as Thebes' protector, a city that can legitimately lay claim to his loyalty as his mother city, a city that in the *Oedipus Tyrannus* he destroyed himself to save. Even Oedipus' fury at Thebes' intention to settle him only on the boundary of the city, not on Theban soil, is hard to understand from the perspective of one kind of order, since there is no denying the fact that he is guilty of incest and patricide and is therefore a polluted being whose presence on his native soil is forbidden by law.

In all of these conflicting perspectives, or ways of ordering action, Oedipus moves with a kind of moral certainty, even as he is engaged in the ebb and flow around him. First, he explains in detail the incorrectness of the chorus's, and later Creon's, understanding of his past actions. The self-blame that led him, at the time of his discovery of those crimes, to blind himself has been replaced by a clear-sighted understanding of his own essential innocence, grounded in his ignorance of what he was doing. This self-understanding does not make him any less aware that he is a polluted being—he does almost forget when he tries to take Theseus' hand, but he then stops himself, Sophocles' clever way of dramatizing his awareness. But it does allow Oedipus to draw a distinction between an internal state and an external one, the first dependent on his own sense of himself, the second determined by the laws and judgments of society.

When Creon tries to shame him into returning to Thebes by depicting him as one who can never escape his crimes, whose presence in the world is an affront to others, he tries to persuade not only Oedipus but the chorus and the audience to see Oedipus as the sum of his actions and what people say about them. For a character in a play, and for the Greeks of this time, that definition of what constitutes a person is not obviously inadequate. Like characters in a play, who can be known only by what they do and say in front of an audience, Athenians thought of themselves as fully defined by the way others viewed their actions and received their words. Oedipus' insistence on something like a conscience, achieved over long years by learning to draw a distinction between who he is and what he has done, between the identity society gives him and his sheer physical existence in the world, is the center of his moral authority. The notion of an internal monitor, guided by the integration of thought, feeling, and action—a sense of a person's moral self separate from conformity to the laws and expectations established by society—is a new development in the Greeks' sense of the individual, one to be fully realized only in the next century by Socrates' student, Plato. But it is at the heart of Sophocles' intuition in this play about the gift that Oedipus has to offer Athens, and the *Oedipus at Colonus* has to offer its audience.

Even Theseus, whose immediate acceptance of Oedipus, based on his own experience as an exile, seems to reveal a man of deep understanding, shows the limit of his point of view in comparison to Oedipus. He concludes his acceptance of Oedipus with the words "For I know / I'm a man, and know / I've no greater claim on tomorrow than you." (627–29/567–68). Here he shows an understanding of the relative extent of his own power, an understanding that leads him immediately to want to protect the suppliant Oedipus. But later, when Oedipus warns him that this acceptance will bring his city into conflict with Thebes, at this time Athens' close ally, Theseus cannot understand how that could come about. His belief in the permanence of the laws of his city and the alliances it constructs with other cities prevents him from seeing the same limit to his city's power that he sees in himself. Yet for the audience, in their current political situation, that limit is all too distressingly apparent. This incomprehension evokes from Oedipus one of the great speeches of the play, in which he points out to Theseus the inevitable pattern of change and transformation that underlies all aspects of human life and that goes to the heart of the limit of human power:

> Dearest son of Aegeus, none but the gods
> escape old age and death; all else
> time in its relentless flood sweeps away.
> The strength of earth and of the body fades,
> trust dies and distrust flourishes,
> and the same spirit never endures
> between friend and friend, city and city.
> For some now, for others later,
> joy becomes bitter, then bitterness joy.   (671–79/607–15)

Essential, then, to the kind of understanding Oedipus has, giving him the ability to judge both himself and others, is an awareness of the fundamental impermanence of the natural and constructed world in which humans live. In the face of that impermanence, the challenge is to find the solid ground on which to base the choices we make and the actions we perform. Oedipus' understanding of change and loss does not make him *feel* the loss any less—when Antigone and Ismene are taken from him he is in despair—but it gives him an unerring sense of how actions conform to and violate the rhythms that constitute the fragile fabric of human order. A man who has wandered without a home for years, who has believed himself the son of two different sets of parents, who has been the savior and destroyer of his city, he makes manifest, in his unmoving position on his rock, the certainty that arises out of radical uncertainty, the capacity to know the continuity in flux, and the moral understanding that the endless years of living as an outcast in the eyes of the world with the knowledge of his own innocence has brought him.

His uncompromising moral sense emerges clearly and shockingly in his encounter with his son. In Oedipus' explanation to Theseus of the wrong Polyneices has done to him, he describes not only the way his sons did nothing to prevent his exile—a fate that the Greeks viewed as a living death—but argues that the timing of the exile was a particular affront because it violated the change in his own understanding of his guilt, which the passage of time had brought him. As he came to see that his guilt was only to have physically committed the acts of murder and incest, not to have worked knowingly for the destruction of his parents, the limit of his blame became clear to him, and he no longer felt the need to go into exile. He was content to remain isolated in his own home. The city's move to exile him, and his sons' passivity, took no account of his changed understanding. Oedipus' sense of the proper timing of things is another aspect of his understanding of the natural rhythm of change as a manifestation of an unchanging order, and it is through Oedipus that we understand something of what it means to be in tune with both.

When Ismene brings him word of the oracle's prediction of the value of his tomb, he says: "So when I am no longer, then I'm a man?" (428/393), pointing to the paradoxical disparity between what humans consider the "prime of life" and that other rhythm his life illustrates. His sense of urgency about Theseus' arrivals throughout the play is the product of his knowledge that the moment when he can reveal the precise facts of his gift to Theseus is not within his control, while Theseus is fully immersed in the self-created rhythms of his political life. At the end of the play the thunder and lightning and the voice of a god saying "Why / do we put off our departure like this? What / a long delay you're making!" (1800–1802/1627–28) are dramatic manifestations of that larger order at work in Oedipus' life. The human experience of that rhythm is the passage of time—"the long companionship of time," as Oedipus says in his opening speech—which for someone like Oedipus has brought a fuller sense of the meaning of his actions. He charges both Creon and Polyneices with violating that rhythm, Creon when he offers to take him back to Thebes, long after his desire to do so has disappeared, and Polyneices when he allowed his exile, although Oedipus understood that it was no longer a necessity.

But Oedipus' cursing of Polyneices is based not only—not largely, even—on Polyneices' ignorance of the changes that time brings, although Polyneices himself points to his guilt here: "To my shame I've come too late / to see all this. . . . But since Compassion / shares the throne with Zeus in all he does, / let her stand beside you also, father— / for the wrongs that are done have some cure / and they're over now, there'll be no more of them" (1385–93/1264–70). His claim that the damage is reparable perhaps indicates the shallowness of his understanding of the rhythm of change, but Polyneices' real crime is his violation of the one unchanging, inalienable fact of human existence: the relationships of blood. They are the only thing that neither time nor circumstance nor human will can change, as Oedipus discovered to his enormous cost as a young man when his true parentage was revealed to him. What Oedipus sees is that Polyneices' knowing repudiation of his father to secure his own political future removes from Polyneices the only unchanging reality a human being has: the bond of children to those who gave them life. This violation is unforgivable in Oedipus' eyes because that unchanging relationship provides a stability that is the basis of human order and moral understanding.

The strongest challenge to Oedipus' point of view comes from his daughter Antigone: "he is your child; show him / some understanding. Other men have bad children / and feel deep anger; but rebuked / by the gentle appeals of those dear to them, / they soften their hearts" (1312–16/1192–1194). Although Antigone's plea for compassion is enough to persuade Oedipus to allow Polyneices into his presence, it has no power to stop Oedipus from cursing him. Here finally we understand why Oedipus belongs in the grove of the Eumenides, the unforgiving goddesses who punish violation of family bonds. Oedipus puts a human face on that absolute judgment, one that comes from his deepest understanding of the impermanence of human existence and the moral need for humans, living within the flux of things, to keep their bearings by paying attention to the one unchanging fact of our existence. Oedipus' earlier discovery, despite his lived experiences, of the ineluctable truth of his true parentage and the profound disorientation that resulted from his (unwilling) ignorance of that truth, makes him deeply aware of the way it must anchor people's experience; his years of wandering, living in the constant movement of exile, have taught him the enormous difficulty of being fully human in the world without that anchor. It is the combination of living through the two extremes of these experiences that makes him uniquely able to judge the way others deal with the tension between the stability and change of a human life. The episodes, which bring the Citizen of Colonus, Ismene, Antigone, Theseus, and Creon within the sphere of Oedipus' judgment, culminate in this encounter between father and son. Oedipus obliterates the kind of future for himself that men try to gain through their sons in order to secure for Athens his guiding spirit. He condemns his son to death for the failure to establish for himself the necessary moral framework in which to act—based on an understanding of what cannot change and what must change, and he bequeaths to Athens the protection of his own understanding.

SOPHOCLES' GIFT TO ATHENS

Oedipus' sense of the inviolability of the blood relationship of child to parent may give him the power of a Fury, but the protection that Oedipus will offer Athens after his death comes not from that power alone but from the combination of impotence and power that makes him so paradigmatically human. That impotence is manifest not only in his beggarly appearance, blindness, and dependence, but also in the moment of his greatest power, when he curses his son. Although Oedipus' language has the force to make believable that his curse will be fulfilled (as we know from myth and from Sophocles' *Antigone*, it is), he does not have control over all the consequences of that curse. After the curse, Antigone and Polyneices have a conversation in which Antigone tries to persuade Polyneices not to pursue the war against his brother. Polyneices, as if already bound by the curse, can see no alternative to walking straight into the disaster he knows awaits him at Thebes. In this moment he provides an interesting contrast to his father in the *Oedipus Tyrannus*, who, when he received an oracle saying he would kill his father and marry his mother, did everything he could to avoid what the oracle predicted and later pursued indefatigably the truth of what he had done. Polyneices' willingness knowingly to sacrifice his army and allies, while keeping them in ignorance, subtly offers evidence for the connection between his treatment of his father and his moral helplessness. He is unable to know the moment when he must act in keeping with, or in defiance of, the opportunities that present themselves. But he does ask Antigone to bury his body, after he is killed, and Antigone promises to do so. She thus binds herself to the fate we see played out in the *Antigone*, which Sophocles deliberately evokes here. So Oedipus' curse on his son is the indirect but nonetheless effectual cause of Antigone's death; yet on the very grounds he curses his son he wishes absolutely to protect his daughter. This he cannot do. The combination of Polyneices' passivity in the face of his father's anger, Antigone's will to act out of her love for her family (the mirror image of Polyneices' weakness), and her move away from the protecting influence of Oedipus' cult at Athens back to Thebes, with which the play ends, are all part of the web of change and flux in human life that will continue after Oedipus' death and that he cannot stop or control.

But the most vibrant and constant evidence of Oedipus' extraordinary combination of weakness and strength, and of his awareness of the double rhythm of the human and divine order, comes from his language, as is only fitting in a form of theater that was as dependent on the spoken word as Greek theatre was (see pp. 23–27). Oedipus has an extraordinary range of expression: from inarticulate cry to authoritative argument, from song to speech, from command to pleading, from curse to blessing, from expressions of hatred to those of love, from anger to gratitude, from teaching to questioning. And beyond this he shows a clear understanding of a kind of speech that outlasts the moment of speaking (which perhaps is of particular importance for the effect that Sophocles hopes to create with the performance of the play itself). This kind of speech is embodied in the secret words that he passes on to Theseus, which he promises will teach "things / which age can never spoil" (1673–74/1519), words that are to be repeated only once in a lifetime, when Theseus, and then another in each generation, passes them on at the moment of death. It is embodied in the curse, which will work its power long after the words themselves have faded. And it is to be found in Oedipus' words that outlast his death, as the Messenger reproduces his final speech to his daughters as a direct quote rather than reported speech, thus recreating Oedipus' voice after his death and perpetuating the power of his speech.

In Oedipus' mouth that most provisional and momentary act, the act of spoken communication (it is important to remember that this tragedy was composed to be viewed only once), has also a permanence that defies the fragility of sound. What is common to the whole range of Oedipus' expression is its authority, the sense that the language comes from the depth of his understanding and the integrity of his thought, feeling, and action. It is unlike the speech of all the other characters in the play, whose words inevitably reveal also their limits. Ismene, for example, will not tell of her experience in traveling to find Oedipus because she does not want to experience the pain of it again. Antigone speaks consistently and exclusively out of her feeling for her father and her brother and is persuasive and effective as far as that feeling goes, but her speech (and her action) expresses no other dimension of character. Theseus, too, is limited in the range of what he can express, as his speech always conforms to his political consciousness and the role he must play within the polis. Polyneices fears to speak at all without some indication of his father's good will. When Antigone persuades him to speak despite Oedipus' silence, he delivers a plea to Oedipus to become his ally in the form of a catalogue of the six other leaders who have joined him in his attack on Thebes. On many levels this catalogue betrays the poverty of Polyneices' language: although it is a standard part of the story of the "Seven against Thebes," it is strangely out of place here, when Polyneices' appeal to Oedipus cannot be made on the basis of an "epic" portrayal of the battle he is about to fight; the audience knows that all six leaders die at Thebes, so it also sounds like an epitaph before the fact; and for Oedipus, so far removed for years from the context in which these names would have meaning, it is meaningless. Like his sense that he has no choice but to fulfill his father's curse, this speech marks Polyneices' disorientation from the moral necessity of the moment.

The most striking contrast to Oedipus' speech comes from Creon, whose insincerity is apparent from the moment he opens his mouth. Since Ismene has given Oedipus and the audience the information that Creon will be coming to try to inveigle Oedipus back to Thebes— not to bring him home but to control his power on Thebes' border— Creon's words are judged from the start by that knowledge. All the arguments he uses—his appeal to Oedipus' loyalty to Thebes, his claims of respect for Athens, his sense of shame about Antigone's and Oedipus' state, and his desire to hide them away in their home—are all colored by the irony created by his hiding his true motive and our knowing it. Polyneices, by contrast, who comes for the same reason, is quite open about his motivation: "Because—if we're to believe the oracles— / the power lies with those who have you / as their ally" (1460–62/1331–32). But Creon tries to gain this goal by the force of his entirely rhetorical arguments, and when they fail he resorts to force, the most definitive evidence of the emptiness of his words, in contrast to Oedipus'. (And his force turns out to be as empty as his words, when the kidnapping of the girls is reversed within minutes of its happening.)

Oedipus' words, by contrast, are untouched by this kind of irony, an irony that Sophocles used so effectively in the *Oedipus Tyrannus* to reveal the limit of Oedipus' understanding. Like the arc of Oedipus' transformation from helpless blind beggar to guide and benefactor of Athens, his language is able to reflect the full range of human experience and, beyond that, his double consciousness of the world of change in which humans live and that larger order with its own rhythm that humans only glimpse, in oracles and seemingly random interventions in the course of their lives.

The power that Oedipus' lived experience and understanding give his language is somehow captured in the Messenger's speech, which reports his last moments. Although the speech is a narrative of what took place, the account moves three times into direct quotation of Oedipus' words and once into quotation of a god's voice addressing Oedipus directly. By this means Sophocles draws an analogy—but only an analogy—between the human and divine voices. The first of Oedipus' words are addressed to Ismene and Antigone in response to their weeping:

> Children, on this day you have no father.
> All that was my life is destroyed on me now:
> You won't ever again have to labor for me
> or look after me as you've always done.
> I know, children, what a hard life it's been.
> But there's one thing can dispel it all,
> one word is enough to wipe hardship away:
> Love, that this man had for you—no man
> can love you more. And now the two of you
> must go on living the rest of your lives
> without him.   (1780–90/1611–19)

Oedipus acknowledges the pain both of the loss his death will bring to his daughters and the hardship that living in the world as he has done has caused them—the constant instability and struggle that is an extreme version of the flux of all human life. And he also offers them an expression of the one unchanging truth, the love their life together has created, which is the flip side of his hatred for his sons and their betrayal of that truth. In the second speech the Messenger quotes, he binds Theseus with a promise to do his utmost to protect his daughters: "give these children / the pledge of your hand" (1806–7/1632). Here his language acts, as it did in his curse, to overcome its impermanence and fashion a future beyond his death (which we know, from Antigone's story, cannot fully succeed—here is the limit of Oedipus' power.) And finally, he orders his daughters to leave with the words "you must be brave now, / and go away from this place, / and not judge it right to see what's forbidden / or hear men say what must not be heard" (1817–20/1640–42). His final gift—the secret of his death-place—belongs only to Theseus, the words that must not be spoken, that somehow come into contact with an order beyond the human, which human language can approach only by silence.

It is tempting to see the Messenger's report of Oedipus' words as a metaphor for Sophocles' gift to Athens on his death: this play. Sophocles knows that the life of his city will have to change, as all human forms must, and change perhaps radically with the end of the war. But his play captures not only what does not change—the bonds we create with each other that can and must be protected against violation—but also the way we can (with time, experience, character, and openness to the world of change, an ability to learn and listen) come to know simultaneously the rhythm of that change and the rhythm of what is beyond our comprehension but that we experience as "the steady sway of some shaping power" (1977/1779). And in the internalization of this knowledge, Oedipus, and the *Oedipus at Colonus*, give us the model for the constancy of self that survives every change in political and social fortune.

Vassar College   RACHEL KITZINGER

CONVENTIONS OF THE ANCIENT
GREEK THEATER

Much of the original experience of Sophocles' audience is lost in encountering a play like the *Oedipus at Colonus* in English instead of Greek and on the page instead of on the stage. Not only is a great deal communicated by the spatial relationships, the physical gestures, the vocal intonations of the actors and the chorus, and the subtleties particular to the Greek language that are so different from those of English, but the conventions of the ancient theater are so different from our own that we cannot even be confident of the way our imaginations may provide the missing aspects of performance as we read. To orient readers to some aspects of the ancient theater that are particularly important for an understanding of this play, I include here a brief summary of the more important aspects of ancient theater production, as far as we can reconstruct them.

The plays performed in the city of Athens for the City Dionysia, as this one was, took place in the open-air theater of Dionysus, on the southern slope of the Acropolis in the spring. The festival was a great civic occasion, lasting five days. It included, among other things, three days of theatrical contest (or four when the city was not at war). On each of these three days a poet would present three tragedies and a satyr play, followed, in wartime, by a comedy written by a different poet. In times of peace, an extra day was added for the performance of the comedies. The fifteen plays presented in this way were performed once and once only. On very rare occasions a play would be awarded a rerun, sometimes years after its original single performance. The City Dionysia was attended by all sectors of the population of Athens, as well as visitors from elsewhere, and all civic business was suspended during the festival. The poets who competed in the festival were thought of as teachers, and the plays performed were an important element in the creation of Athenian civic identity.

Although the stone structures of the theater of which one can still see some remains date from a period later than the performances of the fifth century, the basic elements of the fifth-century theater, which were made of wood, can be largely reconstructed. The seats for the audience of 15,000 to 17,000 climbed up the south slope of the Acropolis in a semi-circular arrangement. At the base of the seats, on ground level, was the circular orchestra, which may have had an altar at its center. This was the space in which the chorus performed. There is more uncertainty about the space used by the actors. A likely probability—but only that—is that the actors moved freely between the orchestra and a slightly raised rectangular stage, impinging on the orchestra on its southern edge. Behind the stage rose the skene, which provided the backdrop for the action. We know nothing of the form of the skene at this point in its evolution except that it was a wooden building with a central doorway and a flat roof from which actors, especially those appearing as gods, could deliver lines. In most plays the skene represents a palace, and the central door is one of three ways of entering and exiting the stage. The other two are the *eisodoi*, passageways on stage right and left, between the skene and the edge of the seating. In any given play the right and left *eisodoi* are consistently associated with the direction to different places relevant to the play. In the *Colonus*, for example, one *eisodos* leads to Thebes, the other to Athens, and the central door represents the pathway into the grove of the Eumenides.

These are the basic elements of the physical theater. There was no lighting—performances took place in daylight—and minimal scenery (what there was took the form of painted panels that could be applied to the front of the skene to change it from a palace to another venue). In the *Colonus*, paintings probably transformed the skene into the grove of the Eumenides. Other objects can also help to set the scene. In this play, for example, the statue of the horseman Colonus would have marked the whole theatrical space as Colonus; in addition there would have been two rock seats for Oedipus, one right up against the skene, which would be understood to be in the grove; the other at the edge of the stage, which would be understood to be just outside the grove. For this play marking those boundaries for the audience is important; these kind of emblematic spatial arrangements are an important dynamic that props create in the ancient theater.

The abstracted physical symbol that the stage can become even stretches, to a certain extent, to the physical presence of the actors. The theater is so large that audience members sitting in the back reaches of the theater are seeing tiny figures below them, over a hundred yards away. Clearly, the effect of the play does not depend on the audience's being able to read minute shifts in body language and facial expression to project the complex idiosyncrasies of a personality, as Western theatrical experience leads us to expect. The actors on the Athenian stage wore masks and elaborately decorated costumes that often covered the whole body. This allowed the three male actors who made up the speaking cast to play multiple roles, both male and female. In this play, for example, the third actor probably came on as the Citizen, Ismene, Theseus, Creon, and Polyneices. In this theatrical situation the words each character delivers give that character a very specific and articulated presence, but the physical appearance is, to a large degree, "generic." The resulting combination lends characters in Greek tragedy compelling paradigmatic force: they are both textured and particular enough to be emotionally compelling, but they are also people involved in making decisions and acting them out in a process and with consequences that any member of the audience—and particularly the male citizens—can see as instructive. Since the setting of the play is almost without exception in the mythical past, and the plot is derived from myth and therefore, in general outline, known to the audience, the experience that the audience has is not derived from the unfolding of the plot per se. Rather, the intensity of the language and the conflicts it plays out combined with the critical distance inherent in the physical circumstances of the theater and the focus on the mythical past creates a theatrical experience that excites, through the imagination, both feeling and thought. The effect of this experience has real consequence for the audience members' understanding of the role they must play in the running of a civic society.

The language of the play was also far from the kind of realistic communication that we are used to. Exchanges between actors are composed in an iambic rhythm, a regular alternation of syllables of shorter and longer duration, usually twelve syllables to a line. Since Greek also had a pitch accent, the sound of these rhythmic lines would to our ear seem more like chanting than conversational speech. The chorus's songs (referred to as odes, or *stasima*) vary in their rhythms, almost all of which are taken from earlier choral lyric traditions. The fifteen chorus members sing the odes, and their rhythms determine the choreography of the dance that the chorus members perform as they sing. The songs were accompanied by a double-reed wind instrument, called an *aulos*, which had particular associations with the worship of the god Dionysus. The play is structured by an alternation between episodes delivered in the iambic rhythm, the poetic rhythm the Greeks considered closest to the rhythm of everyday speech, and choral odes, and were thus multimedia productions. Occasionally, the chorus and an actor sing together, in responsion not unison (a *kommos*), or the actor performs a solo song. The chorus leader also exchanges iambic lines with actors during the episodes. The language of tragedy—its diction and sentence formation—is, as far as we can tell, more stylized than that of everyday speech, although there are traditions familiar to the audience from their everyday life that influence tragic forms of speech: for example, arguments delivered in law courts or the public assembly and songs sung in celebration of a god or to accompany certain kinds of work or on ritual occasions such as weddings. The fact that most of the audience did not use a written form of language in the regular course of their lives and were therefore completely attuned to the spoken word made them sophisticated and subtle receivers of the complex poetic language in which the plays were composed.

The actors and the chorus also, of course, used their bodies to communicate to the audience. Although they had to face the audience more or less frontally to project their voices to the back of the theater, the use of large, expressive gestures, choreography that mimed the images of the songs, the angles of the actors' heads and the subsequent shifts in shading on the mask, and the positioning of bodies in relation to each other had great iconic power in the physical space of the theater and created a dynamic complement to the effect of the words. In this play, for example, it is easy to imagine the communicative significance of the simple act of Oedipus' rising from the stone on which he has been sitting throughout the play and walking without help into the central door of the skene to the accompaniment of thunder (they used a thunder machine) to bring the play to its concluding moments.

Perhaps the greatest difference—among many—between this theater and many contemporary theatrical traditions is the function the plays performed in creating civic identity. The production was paid for by wealthy citizens as a form of taxation; the festival was run and carefully controlled by Athenian magistrates; various rules were established to ensure that the contest between the three playwrights who competed at the festival was as fair as possible; the judges who chose the winner were selected by lot from citizenship rolls; young male citizens performed as the choruses of the plays; and the penalty for anyone disrupting or corrupting the festival's procedures was death. Why did the city expend so much energy on what is to us a form of entertainment? Not only was the theater festival a form of worship of the god Dionysus and thus had strong religious dimensions to it, but the content of the plays dramatized, in a mythical setting, contemporary issues that were very important for citizens and others members of the community of

Athens to think about and debate. The combination of the emotional power of the plays and the formal and abstract qualities of their production effectively engaged the audience in a unique combination of emotional and intellectual turmoil that generated serious thought and debate. The conflicts of the plays revolve around issues that were essential for members of the community to struggle to understand and to debate with each other. The familiarity of the stories, which formed both the informal and formal basis of every citizen's education, gave the audience the opportunity to encounter themselves and rethink their collective identity. And the ambiguities and unresolved conflicts, the ironies and multiple points of view that the play gives voice to gave the citizens whose decisions and actions governed the state—and its empire—an intense awareness of the difficult process of taking action in complex human situations.

Vassar College   RACHEL KITZINGER

ON THE TRANSLATION

Theoretically, it is impossible. One has to try.
W. H. AUDEN, on translation

Translators should probably say nothing about their work, since whatever they say will most likely sound defensive or, at best, like special pleading. Ideally, the translation should speak for itself, embodying the translator's particular "theories" (too specific a word for what are so often ad hoc determinations, choices of a moment and determined by many factors, including personal taste and linguistic capacity), rather than making them explicit. For if they are explicit they open themselves distractingly to opposition and/or dismissal as either betraying the original in unforgivable ways or as simply inadequate. Still, a little foreword is probably useful, if only to suggest that the translation has been performed by someone with opinions and certain commitments, and not by a value-neutral machine.

Echoing the title of a poem by Yeats ("The Fascination of What's Difficult"), one of the most accomplished and satisfying modern translators of the *Oedipus at Colonus* speaks of "the fascination of what is, strictly speaking, impossible." (One has only to consider the dynamically operatic pitch- and cadence-play of the original Greek, impossible to duplicate in English, to recognize the truth of this more or less universal sentiment.) What Robert Fitzgerald (whose edition of the play first appeared in 1941, revised 1956) was referring to was the translator's obligation to write in "the English of Sophocles," remembering, I guess, Holderlin's pithy ambition as a translator of Pindar "to write Greek in German." This present version tries to perform the same impossible task. For me, it has been a task made easier (if no less impossible) by the fact that it is the result of a collaboration with Rachel

Kitzinger, whose exacting lexical and semantic scrupulosity, as well as her scholarly and practical knowledge of the play's language, dramaturgy, and relevant contexts made it possible or at least more plausible for me, lacking knowledge of the language, to attempt this task of translation (what Ezra Pound calls "a thankless and desolate undertaking") in the first place.

What Rachel and I have tried for is a readable and, more important, a speakable text. In doing that, we have not wanted a transformation into a contemporary colloquial manner—inventing an English that would be out of tune with the plain dignity and rhythmic buoyancy, speed, and at the same time solidity of the original. Instead, we have sought an idiomatic English without either antiquarian effects, on the one hand, or too contemporary, colloquial a feel, on the other. To speak only for myself, my purpose was to remain as true as I could to what she offered as the literal (and/or possible) meanings of the words, the lines, and the speeches, while at the same time trying to enact these meanings in an English that had the capacity to be plain, blunt, passionate, and lyrical by turns: to be an instrument capable of conducting an exchange of information, managing an outburst of anger or grief, directing a narrative tale. In addition, I wanted it to be capable of ascending in as natural a manner as possible to a register of something nearer song or chant than "ordinary" speech—as it has to do (in different ways) in the choruses and in those various moments where, in Sophocles' text, the characters themselves shift from the register of speech to that of metrical song.

And while I might have imagined an Irish-accented countryman speaking the lines of the Citizen at the start and the Messenger at the end, and imagined a smoothly (if sinisterly) fluent Creon, a solidly rational Theseus, a young, "heroic," and confused Polyneices, an emotionally quick and sympathetic Antigone, a chorus more tense and ritualized than any character, and an Oedipus as volatile in his self-certain mood-swings as Lear or Prospero, none of these imaginings (phantom voices in my head) prompted me to turn any of Sophocles' *personae* into an idiosyncratic speech manner. What I sought in the end was a language that might achieve a different level of rhythmic intensity as it moved from character to character and from episode to episode, neither ascending to too-obviously rhetorical heights nor descending into overly colloquial, contemporary familiarity. In that way, I hoped that anyone who had to speak the lines on stage or radio would feel neither embarrassment nor disgust. The intention was to compose a "literary script" capable of being competently acted or read with pleasure.

I have not, however, tried to make the choral odes, epodes, or the choral dialogues "songs" in any overt way. (Although an imaginative composer/choreographer could perhaps give the odes, in particular, some effective musical accompaniment. Yeats's Chorus, for example, with anachronistic Yeatsian bravura, chanted in the Gregorian mode.) While Fitzgerald reluctantly chose rhyme and/or regularly patterned stanzas to do this work for him, this seemed to me to sacrifice the strangeness and speed of the Greek to a very different and more light-weight (and over-regulated) kind of lyrical effect. And Robert Fagles' choice (in his 1982 edition) to give the choruses an obviously lyrical *content*, but in free verse lines that have little appeal to the ear, also seems to me to miss something of the Greek effect, its rhythmic and sonic sense of ritualized utterance. What I have done is try to make the expression of these parts of the play different in effect from the various extended speeches and stichomythic passages. I have done this by giving them what I hope is a more pronounced lyrical feel and rhythmic presence than the roughly iambic/roughly pentameter/ roughly natural speech pattern of the rest. (I reiterate "roughly" here, since I haven't tried anywhere in the play to establish a consistency of any English meter nor to duplicate the metrics of the original, either of which choices would ensure, at least for me, spectacular failure. In fact, in the latest drafts, I chose to loosen considerably the sense of the line, unsettling its—even phantom—iambic beat and lengthening or shortening it as the sense and speech occasion seemed to demand.) In the choral parts of the play, however (whether belonging solely to the chorus or shared with one or more characters), I have tried to enhance the sense of the rhythmic unit of the *line*, whereas in the passages of speech the rhythmic sense of the line is more absorbed—though I hope not too diluted—by the sense units of the *sentences*. This accounts in the "song" passages for the deliberate elimination of most punctuation, for the lines being slightly indented, and for their being set in italics. The aim, whatever the outcome, was to give a separate rhythmic feel to these choral utterances (and to those passages where, in the original, the characters move into metric song), thinking this might help the director of a production (whether a performance on stage or on radio) to realize this unique and, for a contemporary audience, perhaps strangest element in the drama as a whole.

One other choice needs a brief word. Whenever I read a translation of a Greek play, I always feel that the expressions of passionate distress (in Greek, *oimoi*, *oimoi talaina*, *pheu pheu*, and other such ejacula-tions), which seem to me simply full-throated utterances of emotion— acoustic units of pure feeling rather than explicitly semantic units—

are clumsily rendered by phrases such as, "Alas!" or "Misery!" or even "Oh!" or "Ah!" or some variants of these. So to translate *oimoi* as "Alas!" in fact weakens rather than strengthens the emotional effect, makes bland and prissily mannered what should be passionate, unleashed, extra-lexical. English is peculiarly poor in these ejaculative bits of diction—words that are emotive sounds. (Only in comic books, the convention being intact, do they appear with any frequency or conviction—where Ugh! Aaargh!, and so on are part of the convention.) In her translation of the *Electra*, Ann Carson deals with this problem by leaving such utterances (often in that play the cries and screams of its heroine) in their Greek form. While we found this an interesting strategy, and not without theatrical possibility, such a choice finally seemed too arbitrary, the sudden invasion of the English text by these Greek words too unnatural, too much of the wrong kind of surprise. The choice we came to, therefore, was two-fold: to substitute a stage direction at these points, stating *With a loud groan* or *With a cry of terror* or *With a wail of despair* and following it with a more or less innocuously generic *Ohhh!* or *Aaahhh!* Each of these then needs to be, in performance, rhythmically integrated into the relevant passage. This passes on to the actor and director the task of inventing the particular register of vocal utterance to fit the particular moment, one that belongs to the production in question. The reader, meanwhile, is not irritated by the use of old-fashioned locutions such as "Alack!" or "Alas!" That, at least, is the intention. As with other aspects of translation, it is at best an imperfect solution to a problem that seems, finally, insoluble.

When Ezra Pound speaks (in the *Cantos*) of "the hard Sophoclean light," he refers both to meanings (those poignantly difficult truths enunciated and, more generally, summoned into being by the plays in their text and performance) and to style. For all the interrogative shadows inherent in its moral implications, there is always an unflinching clarity in Sophocles' expression, a clarity of expression that lets us experience not only the most difficult human facts of physical, earthbound existence—hate, betrayal, and violence as well as love, loyalty, and tenderness—but also the ineffable, ineluctable presence of mystery. Of course, such "functional clarity" (as William Arrowsmith called it), in two plays centered on a blind man's painful pilgrimage into the light, is peculiarly appropriate both as theme and as medium. In the *Oedipus at Colonus* (a play that takes place in the here and now of last things; that begins with a particular question and ends with a universal assertion), both the mysterious and the mundane are equally bathed in this hard light, and it is something of this clarity that I've tried to convey in the translation. I am, in other words, trying to make sure that the language I've used doesn't get in the way of the dramatic content by drawing undue attention to itself.

In Sophocles' text, moreover, such clarity endures despite a range and a fabric of allusion that form a large part of the play's texture and its semantic implication. Both Rachel Kitzinger and I agreed that these allusions should be held on to in the translated version and neither softened (by explanatory paraphrase) nor erased. Some glossing notes have been included to illuminate such of them (mainly proper names and places) as may especially darken the text for modern readers. We also decided to keep stage directions at a minimum, confining them to entrances, exits, and very occasionally a bare description of an action, where this is necessary to give the reader a minimal sense of what's taking place (when this may not be entirely clear from the text). Such a practice accorded with our sense that what we were providing was a text for readers, yes, but also a text that would be suitable for performance. Had we been over-explicit in our stage directions—attempting to indicate where and how any movements might take place, as well as how an actor might interpret any particular passage or moment— we would be getting in the way of the reader, whose imaginative response risked being limited to our interpretation. Furthermore, there are no surviving stage directions in the original, so any we might add would be of necessity interpretive and ill-suited to a play written under and out of such different theatrical conditions. We decided, therefore, that stage directions, beyond the most rudimentary, were not really our business but rightly the concern of a director interested in giving the play an effective contemporary staging. Our wish is to see the text as a thing in itself, capable of many actual renderings on the stage or in the mind. Being as spare as possible with such directions lets the play as a textual experience possess a fluency that would be damaged by the intrusion of too many and too fussy intrusions on the purely textual action. For this reason, too, we decided to confine to a note those headings that in some editions divide the play into its component Choral Odes—their strophes and antistrophes—and Episodes. Within the text itself, such divisions are only a distraction to the general reader, and without them the play flows much more efficiently and pleasingly as an organic unit.

There's always a collaborative aspect to translation (aside from the obvious one in this present case and in the series to which it belongs). One must take into account—either to quarrel with or to be confirmed by—some at least of one's predecessors. I have mentioned two modern translators whose versions I admire: those of Robert Fagles and Robert

Fitzgerald. Although the formal and interpretive choices made by Rachel Kitzinger and me differ from theirs, often in crucial respects, I still have to acknowledge—as someone knowing almost no Greek—the degree to which their translations became part of my own intellectual and imaginative fodder as a translator engaged in the same "strictly speaking, impossible task." Other nourishment was provided by the Loeb prose version by Hugh Lloyd Jones and the nineteenth-century version by R. C. Jebb. The somewhat freer translation by Paul Roche (1959, revised 1991) was also one I returned to with interest, having admired it (and used it in the classroom) years ago. It remains a lively and imaginative rendering. I decided not to consult the version by Yeats, which is, if memory serves, too free to be useful, as well as, in terms of its rhetoric and its verse, too dominantly Yeatsian to be anything but a fatal temptation to my own ear. It is an enviable recreation—not in "the English of Sophocles," however, but in that, most decisively, of Yeats.

In the end, a translation—indispensable as it may be—is only a version of the original ("versions of possibilities," as Hans Magnus Enzensberger has said). In some ways, it resembles the Messenger's speech in this play, attempting to present in a secondary language what defies explanation or adequate representation. Like the performance of a play or a piece of music, a translation is a "reading" of the given text, and as such is provisional, absolutely provisional. All one can hope for it is that it brings that foreign thing (script, score, text) somehow home to those who encounter it in the new medium, the new language. The Messenger's speech, after all, does let the old men of the Chorus share, at a distance, the ineffable, mysterious facts he has scrupulously witnessed. In our case, the hope is that this version in English brings home to those without Greek or to those English-speakers who may be students of Greek an experience that allows them to feel they have been brought into some enabling contact with the play: that they have had in the reading of it or in attending it as performance (aural or theatrical) some—otherwise unavailable—experience of its inexhaustible presence, sense, and meanings.

Vassar College   EAMON GRENNAN

This translation is based on the Greek text of the play edited by H. Lloyd-Jones and N. Wilson, published by Oxford University Press, 1990. In only a few instances have we chosen an alternate reading.

OEDIPUS AT COLONUS

CHARACTERS

OEDIPUS father and brother of Antigone, Ismene, Polyneices, and Eteocles; husband and son of Jocasta; former king of Thebes but now an exile

ANTIGONE daughter and sister of Oedipus who has accompanied him in his years of exile

STRANGER a citizen of Colonus

CHORUS of elderly citizens of Colonus

ISMENE sister and daughter of Oedipus who has remained in Thebes after Oedipus' exile

THESEUS legendary king of Athens

CREON brother of Jocasta, uncle and brother-in-law of Oedipus

POLYNEICES son and brother of Oedipus, brother of Ismene, Antigone, and Eteocles, son-in-law of King Adrastos of Argos.

A grove near Athens, in the district of Colonus. Entrance, stage left, leads to Athens, entrance stage right to Thebes. The grove stretches across the back of the stage. A large unhewn rock lies just inside the grove. Toward the front of the stage there is a rock ledge. On one side stands an equestrian statue. From the direction of Thebes, enter OEDIPUS *slowly, leaning on* ANTIGONE, *both in ragged clothing. They stop at the unhewn rock in the grove.*

OEDIPUS What country is this? Antigone, child
          of a blind old man: Whose city is it?
          Who'll offer any pitiful gift today
          to wandering Oedipus, the homeless man?
          He asks little and gets less, though even less
          than little is enough—since the long
          companionship of time, and bitter trouble,
          and beyond that the manner I was born to, teach me
          to be easy with whatever happens. But child, if
                you find
          any resting place on this traveled road   10
          or in some grove set apart for the gods, lead me
          and seat me in safety there, so we
          may find out where we are. As strangers
          we've learned how to listen to the natives of a place
          and to act according to what we hear.

ANTIGONE Father, poor Oedipus, unhappy man:
          I can see the roof-towers of the city a long way off,
          but I'm sure this place we're in is holy ground:
          it's thick with olive trees, laurel, and bending vines   20
          and—listen!—nightingales—richly feathered
          and filling the air with their sweet voices.
          Rest yourself. Set down your body
          on this rough rock. For old as you are
          you've been a long time traveling.

OEDIPUS So . . . help me sit down. Mind the blind man!

                                          He sits on the rock.

ANTIGONE   No need to tell me. Time has taught me that.

OEDIPUS   Do you know then, and can *you* teach *me*
               what this place is we've stopped in?

ANTIGONE   I can't. But I know that's Athens over there.

OEDIPUS   Yes. Everyone we met said *Athens* . . . *Athens*.   30

ANTIGONE   Should I go and see what place this is?

OEDIPUS   Do, child, if there's anyone living here.

ANTIGONE   I'm sure there is. . . . But no need to go:
               I see someone; he's not far off.

OEDIPUS   Coming this way? Has he set out in our direction?

                    Enter STRANGER *(citizen of Colonus) from direction*
                                                              of Athens.

ANTIGONE   He's here, father, right beside us. Now ask
               whatever you think fitting for the moment. Here he is.

OEDIPUS   Stranger, this woman, who is my eyes
               as well as her own, says you've come looking
               just in time to enlighten—   40

STRANGER   Not another word! Get up from there—there where
                    you're sitting—
               that's holy ground! It isn't lawful to walk there.

OEDIPUS   What ground? And which gods? Whose sacred place?

STRANGER   It mustn't be entered; no one can live there. It
                    belongs to
               the Goddesses—the daughters of the earth, of
                    the dark!

OEDIPUS What's their name? I'd say a prayer to them if I
                heard it.

STRANGER Here we call them the all-seeing Eumenides. In
                other places
              they rightly have other names.

OEDIPUS May they look on their suppliant kindly—
              for I'll never leave this sanctified place.   50

STRANGER What's that you're saying?

OEDIPUS The password for what's to come.

STRANGER It's not for me to move you without permission from
                the city;
              first, I'll let them know what you're doing.

OEDIPUS For the gods' sake, stranger, beggar as I am—
              don't dishonor me by refusing what I ask.

STRANGER Ask then. I'll tell you what I can. I'll not
                dishonor you.

OEDIPUS What is this place we've come to?

STRANGER Listen, I'll tell you what I know. For one thing,
              every bit of this place is holy: 60
              Blessed Poseidon has a home here,
              and the god who brought us fire, the Titan
                Prometheus.
              That very spot you've stepped into
              we call the bulwark of Athens—this country's
              Bronze-footed Threshold. And all these fields
              were laid out by that horseman there, Colonus,
              and carry their founder's name, and
              the people who live here still hold it in common.
              So you see, stranger, since you ask how it is:
              It's a place made famous by no fine stories,   70

39

only we live together here
and honor the presence of these divinities.

OEDIPUS You say there are people living here?

STRANGER Indeed there are. Bearing this hero's name.

OEDIPUS Have they a ruler? Or are the laws
made by the people themselves?

STRANGER The lord of the city is lord of this place, too.

OEDIPUS Who is this lord of kingly strength and speech?

STRANGER His name, stranger, is Theseus—old King Aegeus's
son.

OEDIPUS Could you send a messenger to him?   80

STRANGER Why? To come and speak to you? For what?

OEDIPUS So, with a small service, he'd gain a great good.

STRANGER What good could a blind man offer?

OEDIPUS Words. When I speak
they will see everything.

STRANGER Do you know, stranger, what you need do now
to be safe here and stay within the law?
I'll tell you, since, in spite of what you've suffered,
I see something noble in you. Stay there,
there where you first appeared, while I   90
go to the citizens (who live *here*, not in the city)
and tell them what's happened. For they will decide
to take you in or send you away.

Exit STRANGER, *in direction of Athens.*

OEDIPUS Has the stranger gone, child?

ANTIGONE He's gone, father; you can tal
There's nobody near—no on

OEDIPUS Dread Ladies, before whose
Since I've brought my body
don't be deaf to my prayers,
        himself, who
when he foretold the horrors that lay ahead   100
said that in the fullness of time I'd find rest
when I reached a country I could stop in at last
in a shelter for strangers, a sanctuary
of the Holy Ones. And I could settle then
my wretched life—for the good of those
who would let me live there, and to the ruin
of those who drove me into exile.
And Apollo said there would be signs:
earthquake or thunder, or the bolts of Zeus
lighting up the sky in flashes. I see now   110
it must have been your sure prompting
led me to this grove, or else
I'd never have come upon you here first—
        my abstinence
matching your rites without wine. And I'd never
have set my body on this holy seat
in the rough rock itself. But now grant me, Goddesses,
in keeping with the voice of Apollo,
some limit, some end
to my life's journey, unless
I seem of little or no account, although   120
I've been subject to greater hardships
than any that have tried any man in the world. Come,
sweet children of the ancient dark! Come,
city of Athens—called the city of Pallas, of
        great Athena;
called the most honored city of all—
show pity for Oedipus; show your pity

41

to this poor phantom of a man. For this, surely,
is not the body I began with.

ANTIGONE Quiet! There are men, old men—
the guardians of this place you've stopped in.   130

OEDIPUS I'll be quiet. Hide me in the grove somewhere,
off the beaten path. Hide me, till I hear
what these men have to say. That
is the kind of knowledge right action depends on.

Enter CHORUS *from direction of Athens.*

CHORUS *Look about you!*
Who was the man? Where is he gone?
What secret spot has he scurried to now?
Seek this rashest most reckless of men!
Shout out loud! Search every corner! Find him!
A tramp—an old tramp—not of this place   140
or he'd never have entered the virgin grove
of these implacable Maidens whose very name
makes us tremble to say it.
So with eyes averted we slip by them in silence
letting them hear without words
the reverence alive in our minds.
But now people say someone's burst in here
showing no fear and no respect.
But though I look all over this godly grove
I still can't see where he's come to rest.   150

OEDIPUS Here! I am he. I am here!
By wordsound, as they say, I see.

CHORUS   *With a rhythmical common cry of horror.*
Aaahhh! Awful the sight of him! Awful his voice!

OEDIPUS I beseech you, don't see in me a lawless man.

CHORUS Zeus protect us! Who is this old man?

OEDIPUS   One whose fortune, protectors of this place,
           wasn't so good that you'd call him blessed.
           Were it otherwise — look! — I'd not be
           making my way with someone else's eyes;
           nor, big man that I am,   160
           anchoring myself on these slight arms.

CHORUS   With a rhythmical common cry of distress.
           Aaaieee! Blind eyes!
           Were you born like this? Born for this?
           It seems you've had a long hard life —
           but you won't bring down this curse of yours
           on us too if I can help it.
           You've gone too far now out of bounds —
           so go no farther in that grassy silent grove
           where bright water in the flowing bowl
           streams into a stream of honey.   170
           Move! Stand off! Step away from where you are!
           Toil-worn wanderer you hear what we say?
           If it's talk you want
           walk off forbidden ground
           and speak your mind where it's lawful for all.
           Until you do that hold your tongue.

OEDIPUS   Daughter, what now? What should we do?

ANTIGONE   Be as careful, father, as those who live here:
           we should yield to what's needed: we should listen.

OEDIPUS   Take hold of me, so.   180

ANTIGONE   Here's my hand. Touching you. Here.

OEDIPUS   Don't let any harm come to me, strangers,
           now I've trusted you and moved as you asked.

CHORUS   *Old man — from this place of rest*
           no one will move you against your will.

43

> In what follows, OEDIPUS moves slowly forward
> from the grove to the rock ledge.

OEDIPUS   *So? Farther?*

CHORUS   *Come a little forward. On. Forward.*

OEDIPUS   *Farther? So?*

CHORUS   *Keep leading him child.*
           Forward. Farther forward. You see what we mean.   190

ANTIGONE   *Come father. Now follow me.*
           With feeble unseeing steps
           follow where I lead you.

CHORUS   *Long-suffering man*
           leaning on a stranger in this strange land:
           be ready to hate what this city's learned to hate
           and to hold in high esteem what it holds dear.

OEDIPUS Child—now lead me,
           so we may stand on lawful ground
           where we may speak, and listen too.   200
           Let us not struggle against necessity.

CHORUS   *Here now. Here. Not a step*
           beyond this rocky platform.

OEDIPUS   *Like this?*

CHORUS   *Yes. Far enough. You hear what we say.*

OEDIPUS   *Should I sit now?*

CHORUS   *Yes—to the side. Set yourself down*
           here at the rock's edge: here.

ANTIGONE   *Dear father let me guide you. It is my task*
           to fit your footstep to my steady step.   210

OEDIPUS   Groans with the effort.
           Ohhh!

ANTIGONE   *Lean your old body on my loving arm.*

OEDIPUS   Groans aloud.
        Ohhh! Ruin! Destruction!

        He sits at the very edge of the rock ledge.

CHORUS   *Suffering man—you're settled now. So speak.*
        What nature were you born to?
        Who's led like this in so much pain?
        What country do you bring news of?

OEDIPUS   *Ah strangers! I have no city. But do not—*

CHORUS   *What is it you forbid old man?*

OEDIPUS   *Do not ask who I am.*   220
        Don't seek. Don't explore. Go no farther.

CHORUS   *Why no farther?*

OEDIPUS   *A terrible birth—*

CHORUS   *Speak! Say!*

OEDIPUS   *Child! What should I say?*

CHORUS   *What seed do you come from?*
        Speak stranger! What father?

OEDIPUS   With a cry of despair.
        Aaahhh me! Aaahhh! Child!
        What suffering is in store for me now?

CHORUS   *Speak since you've come to the very brink.*   230

OEDIPUS   *I'll speak. I've nowhere to hide.*

CHORUS   *Why this holding back? Go on!*

OEDIPUS   *A son . . . you must know . . . of Laius . . .*

CHORUS   With a great groan of distress.
        Aahhh!

OEDIPUS   *. . . the family of Labdacus . . .*

CHORUS   *O Zeus!*

OEDIPUS   *. . . wretched Oedipus—*

CHORUS   *You mean you are he?*

OEDIPUS   *Don't be afraid of all I tell you.*

CHORUS   With a cry of horror.
            Aaahhh!   240

OEDIPUS   *Ill-fated . . .*

CHORUS   With an angry shout.
            Ohhh! Ohhh!

OEDIPUS   *Daughter:*
            what's happening?

CHORUS   *Out! Farther off! Get away from this land!*

OEDIPUS   *But how will you keep your promise then?*

CHORUS   *No man when avenging a wrong—*
            matching one deceit with another
            and giving back not kindness but a blow—
            can rightly receive revenge in return.
            So unanchor from this seat and quit my land   250
            for fear you'd fasten on my city
            some graver obligation.

ANTIGONE   *Ah strangers—men of honor and respect!*
            Though you may not endure this old man my father
            —hearing what he did against his will—
            yet I entreat you strangers to pity me
            for this sad suffering father.
            Appearing like one of your own before you
            I gaze with seeing eyes on your faces
            that this wretched man may win your respect.   260
            Look! In our sufferings
            we depend on you as we depend
            on the power of a god. Come! Show some favor!
            I can't expect to get what I ask
            yet I implore you by whatever you cherish:
            your wife—your child—your land—your god!
            For you know well
            you could never lay eyes on any man
            who could escape if a god leads him.

CHORUS LEADER Know, daughter of Oedipus,   270
because of your fortune we pity you both
in equal measure. Yet we tremble at what the gods
      send us,
and wouldn't have the strength to say
anything we haven't said to you already.

OEDIPUS Then what's become of reputation? What good is
a good name if it fades like morning dew?
What good is it if Athens stands alone, as they say,
a god-fearing city—alone able to save
the sick, afflicted stranger. Where is the good in this
      for me,
seeing—since my name alone makes you tremble—   280
you'll drag me from this sanctuary here
and drive me away? It's not my body you fear
nor what I've done. For know, I suffered
more than ever I acted, as you'd see
if I spoke those things of my father and mother
which make you afraid of me. I'm well aware of this.
But how am I bad in my own nature? I only
returned an action I suffered,
so even had my eyes been wide open
I couldn't, with justice, be accused of wrongdoing.   290
But in *ignorance* I came where I did and
I suffered; but those at whose hands I suffered,
I was *knowingly* destroyed by them.
In light of this, strangers, I am, in the god's name,
your suppliant. Since in your piety
you've made me quit this holy place,
now protect me. Don't honor the gods
and then make light of them. Think
how they look on good men and on bad,
how the unrighteous one never escapes them.   300
Don't darken bright Athens, that happy city,
with unrighteous acts. As here you received me
a suppliant with my pledge, now shield me, now
watch over me. Don't dishonor this body
just because it's hard to look at. For I've come
in reverence, under the gods' protection, to bring

a gift to the citizens of this city. When your leader
gets here, the one you look up to, you'll hear all,
then you'll know everything. Till that happens,
I pray you, do no wrong.   310

CHORUS LEADER Old man, it's impossible not to respect this
grave argument of yours: there's nothing light
about the words you offer. But the lord of this land
will be able to ponder them for us.

OEDIPUS And where is the lord of this land, strangers?

CHORUS LEADER Here in this country, in his father's city.
That look-out who brought us has gone to get him.

OEDIPUS And do you think he'll feel concern for a blind man?
So he'd come himself, in his own person?

CHORUS LEADER Yes—all the more when he knows your name.   320

OEDIPUS But who will bring him that name?

CHORUS LEADER It's a long road: many travelers' tales
wander about on it. When our lord hears, be sure
he'll be here. For your name, old man,
is on all men's tongues; so even if
he's sleeping on some slow journey,
when he hears of you he'll come with all speed.

OEDIPUS Let him come, then, with good fortune
for his city and me. For what good man
is not a friend to himself?   330

ANTIGONE   *Looking toward the entrance from Thebes.*
Oh Zeus! What should I say? Father, what should
I think?

OEDIPUS What, Antigone? What is it, child?

48

ANTIGONE   A woman, coming this way: she's riding
                  a Sicilian pony, and shading her face
                  with a broad-brimmed sun-hat you'd find in Thessaly.
                  What can I say? What *should* I say?
                  Is it she or not? Am I wandering in my mind?
                  I say *Yes!* I say *No!* But I cannot . . .
                  poor wretch, poor woman, *it is!*
                  She draws nearer now, and I can see   340
                  her eyes brightening in a sign of welcome
                  that says—there's no doubt!—it's Ismene!

                              Enter ISMENE *from direction of Thebes.*

                  Ismene herself! Ismene!

OEDIPUS   Child, what do you mean?

ANTIGONE   Your daughter, the sister who shares my blood,
                  she's right here before our eyes!
                  And you'll know it now by the sound of her voice.

ISMENE   Father! Sister! These two names sweetest to my ears!
                  With labor and pain I've found the two of you,
                  and now how painful it is to look at you.   350

OEDIPUS   My child! You've come?

ISMENE   Oh father, father! Poor battered man! Father!

OEDIPUS   My child, you're here?

ISMENE   I've traveled a hard road to find you.

OEDIPUS   Touch me, my child.

ISMENE   I touch you both at once.

OEDIPUS   Ah—children of the same blood.

ISMENE   Look! The wretched clutch of us!

49

OEDIPUS You mean this girl and me?

ISMENE And me, a woeful third.   360

OEDIPUS Daughter, why have you come?

ISMENE For your sake, father.

OEDIPUS Out of longing, is it?

ISMENE And as my own messenger—
along with the only servant I could trust.

OEDIPUS But the young men of our blood—where are they?
What are they doing?

ISMENE They are . . . wherever they are. Terrible
what lies between them now.

OEDIPUS Ach, those two! In their nature, in their way of life,   370
they mimic Egyptian habits. For the men of Egypt
sit indoors weaving, while their wives
go out every day in the world
to provide what they need. So here you both are,
while those fit for the task do housework
like maids. The two of you do their work, this
      hard work—
caring for my suffering self. This girl here,
since she grew from a child into a woman's
      strong body
has tramped through misfortune, leading an old man.
Often barefoot, often hungry,   380
she's crossed wild woodland, and often
under scorching sun or drenching rain
she's toiled in patience, not giving a thought
to home or comfort or food for herself—
so long as her father has enough to eat.
And you, my child [to ISMENE], years ago you reached
      your father
with all those prophecies; traveling in secret

50

so the people of Thebes would know nothing—
all those prophecies about my body. And when I was
driven out in the world, it was you   390
who made yourself my faithful guardian.
And now, Ismene, have you come once more
with some new story for your father? This time
what mission drove you from home? For you've come
for some reason, haven't you, with some fearful news?

ISMENE What I suffered, searching for you, father—
asking where you lived, what life you led—I'll not
        mention,
for I've no wish to feel that pain twice over
in the doing and the telling. But the bad news I've
        brought
concerns those two, your ill-fated sons.   400
At first they were content to surrender
the throne to Creon, and not pollute the city—
        mindful
of the ruin, begun long ago with their ancestors,
which destroyed your unhappy house.
But now—with a god behind it, and willful wildness—
bitter strife has sprung up between these
two thrice-miserable men, each one hungry
for power, each wanting to rule on his own.
The younger, in temper as well as in years, pushes
the older, Polyneices, from the royal throne,   410
exiling him from his fatherland. And now
the tale is on every man's tongue,
that having fled to the hollow plain of Argos
he adopts a new family, makes a warlike alliance,
and plans to conquer his own land of Cadmus
with honor, or fall in battle and fly to the heavens.
This isn't just words, father,
but dreadful deeds. And I don't know how
the gods will pity your bitter troubles.

OEDIPUS Did you hope somehow, some day, the gods   420
would look on me kindly, and I might be
        made whole?

51

ISMENE I did, father. Because of recent prophecies.

OEDIPUS Prophecies, child? What has been prophesied?

ISMENE That the men of Thebes would seek you out one day,
living or dead, to ensure their prosperity.

OEDIPUS Look at me. Who'd be better off because of such
a man?

ISMENE They say their power lies in you. They've found
this out.

OEDIPUS So when I am no longer, then I'm a man?

ISMENE Yes. For now the gods who ruined you
have begun to restore you, to raise you up.   430

OEDIPUS To raise up an old man is a silly business—an
old man
who in his youth took a fall.

ISMENE But because of these prophecies, very soon now,
Creon will be here.

OEDIPUS And means to do what, daughter? Explain it to me.

ISMENE To settle you near the land of Cadmus, so they
can control you, without you crossing their borders.

OEDIPUS What good will they get if I'm lying before their gates?

ISMENE Any harm to your tomb means disaster for them.

OEDIPUS Common sense would tell you that; no need
for a god.   440

ISMENE That's why they wish to keep you
near their land, but with no power of your own.

OEDIPUS   And after I'm dead, will they scatter
          even the shadow of Theban dust over me?

ISMENE   No, father; your father's blood will not allow it.

OEDIPUS   Then they'll never take me into their power!

ISMENE   Then this will be a bitter trouble to the Cadmeians.

OEDIPUS   When, child? What events will come together to bring
          that about?

ISMENE   Your rage, when they stand at your grave.

OEDIPUS   Where have you heard all this, my child?   450

ISMENE   From the envoys who returned from the altars
          at Delphi.

OEDIPUS   And Apollo has spoken such words of me?

ISMENE   That's what they said when they returned to Thebes.

OEDIPUS   Did either of my sons hear any of this?

ISMENE   Both heard it, all of it, and understood it well.

OEDIPUS   And even when they heard all this—wicked men!—
          they let power-hunger come before all feeling for me?

ISMENE   It saddens me to hear you say it, but that's
          my message.

OEDIPUS   Well then, let the gods not quench this
          ill-fated quarrel of theirs! And in the battle
                between them,   460
          which grips them as tightly as they their own spears,
          may the end of it depend on me. Then
          the one who now holds scepter and throne would

not remain in the state he's in, and the one driven out
would never get back. For they neither
guarded nor defended me—me who gave them life!—
when I was driven in dishonor from my
        father's country,
although I was cast out before their eyes
and declared an exile. Will you say the city then
acted fairly, giving me what I craved?   470
No! Again no! What's true
is that in those first days—my spirit in flames
and I longing for the comfort of death, wanting
        the people
to stone me to death—not one man came forward
to grant my wish. But then
when my troubles were no longer young
and I began to see my passion had pushed me too far,
that I'd blamed myself too much for my mistakes,
then, after all that time, the city
chose to use force and drive me out. And they—   480
sons of their father, able to help their father—
were unwilling to act. So, for want of a word,
I became an exile; with their knowledge and consent
a wanderer forever. But these young women—
        innocent
of the world—have given me all they can; from them
I get nourishment, protection, a secure place
without fear, while those men bartered their father
for a scepter's power, to be sole rulers
of that country. But they'll not win
me as an ally, and they'll get no good   490
from their rule in the land of Cadmus.
I know this, for I hear the prophecies
this girl utters, and remember those
once delivered by Phoebus himself. Let them send
Creon, or any other man of power in that city,
to seek me out. For if you, strangers,
along with the Goddesses present in this place,
are willing to defend me, you'll bring
a great savior to your city, and bitter trouble
        to my enemies.

CHORUS LEADER Oedipus, you're a man who deserves our pity,   500
               as these do, your loyal daughters. But since
               you say you're the savior of this land
               I want to advise you for your own good.

OEDIPUS My friend, since you know I'll do all you ask,
         be my guide now and give me good counsel.

CHORUS LEADER You should perform the purification rite
               of those Goddesses whose presence you entered
               and on whose holy ground you walked.

OEDIPUS How should I do it? Teach me, strangers.

CHORUS LEADER First, in purified hands, you should bring   510
               sacred libations from the ever-flowing stream.

OEDIPUS And when I've drawn this undefiled water?

CHORUS LEADER You'll find mixing bowls, made by a cunning
                    craftsman:
               wreathe these bowls on their rims and handles.

OEDIPUS With branches, or woven wool, or some other way?

CHORUS LEADER With the fleece of a newborn lamb, freshly shorn.

OEDIPUS Be it so. And then? How should I finish the ritual?

CHORUS LEADER Facing where the sun comes up, pour your libations.

OEDIPUS With the bowls, then, I should pour my libations?

CHORUS LEADER Exactly, those bowls. There will be three streams.   520
               Let the last bowl flow till it's empty.

OEDIPUS And this last, filled with what? Go on with
              your lesson.

CHORUS LEADER Honey and water. You must not add wine.

OEDIPUS   And when dark-leaved earth receives these libations?

CHORUS LEADER   Place three times nine olive branches on it.
Use your two hands. And say these prayers—

OEDIPUS   I long to hear them: they have great power.

CHORUS LEADER   As we call them Eumenides, the Kindly Ones, pray
they receive their suppliant with a kindly heart
and be his savior. Ask this or let another   530
ask it for you. Pray with unheard words, do not
cry aloud. Then leave backwards, don't turn around.
If you do all this, stranger, I'll risk
standing by you. Otherwise, I'd fear for you.

OEDIPUS   Daughters, do you hear these local people,
                these strangers?

ISMENE   We heard. Now say, you, what has to be done.

OEDIPUS   I can't move on my own; my lack of strength
                and sight
is a twin affliction. But one of you go
and do as they've said. For one living soul, I believe,
is as good as ten thousand to pay the debt   540
fulfilled by this ritual, if that one is there
with good intent. But do it quickly
and don't leave me alone: infirm as I am,
I can't move without a guide.

ISMENE   Father, I'll go to perform this rite.

                                        To CHORUS.
Where is the place it has to be done?

CHORUS LEADER   On the far side of this grove, stranger.
If you need anything, someone there will instruct you.

ISMENE   I'll go and do it. Stay here, Antigone,
and take care of our father. When one labors
                for a parent,   550

one should never remember the trouble—
it shouldn't feel like labor at all.

Exit ISMENE, *through the grove.*

CHORUS   *Stranger: it's terrible to bring to life a pain*
          long laid to rest. Yet I long to ask—

OEDIPUS   *What?*

CHORUS   *About that shattering sorrow you wrestled with—*
          ungovernable as the sea.

OEDIPUS   *I beg by the bonds of hospitality*
          don't recklessly open
          the wounds which to my shame I've suffered.   560

CHORUS   *Told over and over the story's well known.*
          But I'd like the simple truth of it.

OEDIPUS   With a groan.
          Ohhh!

CHORUS   *Be easy I beseech you.*

OEDIPUS   With a gasp of despairing resignation.
          Aahhh! Aahhh!

CHORUS   *Hear me.*
          For I have heard what you desire.

OEDIPUS   *Misery stranger! And as the god is my witness*
          I bore it willingly.
          But nothing that happened was of my choosing.   570

CHORUS   *What was it?*

OEDIPUS   *In a misery-laden bed the city*
          locked me into a ruinous marriage.
          I knew nothing.

CHORUS   *Was it lying with your mother as I hear*
          you filled the bed with the awful name?

OEDIPUS   With a groan.
          Aahh! *Stranger! These words are death.*
          And out of my loins these two girls—

57

CHORUS   *What are you saying?*

OEDIPUS   *This double ruin—*   580

CHORUS   *O Zeus!*

OEDIPUS   *I planted in my mother's shared womb.*

CHORUS   *So they're yours? Offspring and—*

OEDIPUS   *Yes. From one source. Sisters to their father.*

CHORUS   With a cry of horror.
           Aaahhh!

OEDIPUS   *Aaahhh! Indeed! Pain*
           of a million wounds torn open again.

CHORUS   *You've suffered—*

OEDIPUS   *Things not to be forgotten.*

CHORUS   *You did—*   590

OEDIPUS   *No not did!*

CHORUS   *Then what?*

OEDIPUS   *I received a gift for the help I gave.*
           Would I'd never taken it—
           man as I am with a heart that suffers.

CHORUS   *Miserable man what more? You murdered—*

OEDIPUS   *What are you saying? What do you want to know?*

CHORUS   *—your father!*

OEDIPUS   Gives a cry of pain.
           Aaahhh! Wound upon wound! A second blow!

CHORUS   *You killed!*   600

OEDIPUS   *Yes I killed. But on my side—*

CHORUS   *What?*

OEDIPUS   *Some justice.*

CHORUS   *What do you mean?*

OEDIPUS   *I'll tell you what I mean.*
               In the grip of disaster I destroyed and murdered.
               But I came to it innocent in law:
               I knew nothing.

               Enter THESEUS, *from the direction of Athens.*

CHORUS LEADER But look, here's our king: Theseus, son of Aegeus.
               He's come in answer to your message.   610

THESEUS   I've often heard over the years
               of the bloody destruction of your eyes,
               and so I know you, son of Laius.
               And having heard more on my way here,
               I now understand even more,
               for your tattered clothes and shattered face
               tell us who you are. And in pity I'd
               ask you, ill-fated Oedipus, what you want
               of my city and me—you and your ill-fated guide.
               Teach me that. For I know   620
               it would have to be some act beyond telling
               to make me want to turn away. Like you,
               I was raised an exile, far from home,
               and often, on my own, I had to face
               mortal danger. So I could never turn aside
               and not try to save any stranger
               in the state I find you in now. For I know
               I'm a man, and know
               I've no greater claim on tomorrow than you.

OEDIPUS   Your generosity, Theseus, in so few words,   630
               leaves me with little to explain. For you
               are in possession of who I am, who my father was,
               and the country I've come from. There
               is nothing left for me to say—except
               what I desire, and then I'm done.

THESEUS   Teach me that, so I'll know all there is to know.

OEDIPUS   I've come to give you, as a gift, my own
          miserable body. It's little enough to look at,
          but it's worth more than beauty itself.

THESEUS   What makes it worth your coming here?   640

OEDIPUS   In time you may learn that, but not now.

THESEUS   When will this offering come to light?

OEDIPUS   When I die, and you lay out a grave for me.

THESEUS   What you ask for is life's last act. But you forget
          what will happen before that end.
          Or do you think that's of no importance?

OEDIPUS   I do. The last act brings all that with it.

THESEUS   Then it's soon told, this favor you're asking.

OEDIPUS   Mind what you say! This is no small contest!

THESEUS   Do you mean your sons' doings? Or whose?   650

OEDIPUS   All those who'll force me to go back.

THESEUS   But if you went willingly? Exile's no good for you.

OEDIPUS   True. But when I wanted to stay, they refused!

THESEUS   But this is foolish. What good is passion
          in the midst of misfortune?

OEDIPUS   When you hear my story, then give your advice.
          For the moment, let be.

THESEUS   Instruct me, then. I mustn't blame before
                I understand.

OEDIPUS   I've suffered, Theseus. One horror on top of another.

THESEUS You mean the ancient misfortunes of your family? 660

OEDIPUS No! All Greece tosses that story about.

THESEUS Then what greater sickness has a grip on you?

OEDIPUS Here's how it is: by my own flesh and blood
I was driven from my country, and as a father-killer
I can never go back.

THESEUS How could they send for you, then, and still keep you
far off?

OEDIPUS The voice of a god will force them.

THESEUS What sufferings will the oracle make them afraid of?

OEDIPUS That otherwise they must be struck down, here.

THESEUS But how could their rancor spread to me? 670

OEDIPUS Dearest son of Aegeus, none but the gods
escape old age and death; all else
time in its relentless flood sweeps away.
The strength of earth and of the body fades,
trust dies and distrust flourishes,
and the same spirit never endures
between friend and friend, city and city.
For some now, for others later,
joy becomes bitter, then bitterness joy. So
if fair weather is what holds now 680
between you and Thebes, boundless time
in its motion gives birth to nights and days
beyond number, and in their course
this concord between you will grow to discord
over a word, a little word, and war
will shatter it. And where this happens,
my cold corpse—asleep, unseen—will drink
their warm blood, if Zeus is still Zeus,
and his son, Phoebus Apollo, speaks the pure truth.

But hard, secret words like these   690
aren't sweet in the mouth, so leave me
there where I started, and just look after
your own good faith. You'll never say—unless
the gods deceive me—that in this grove
you received in Oedipus a worthless guest.

CHORUS LEADER My lord, for some time now this man
has been making our country promises like this.

THESEUS Indeed? But who would turn away the friendship
of such a man? First, our alliance
always assures us a hearth in common.   700
Then, coming as a suppliant of the gods,
he promises in return, to my country and me,
a great recompense. These are things I respect,
and I'd never spurn what he offers
but offer in return a home in this country.
And if this is the place it now pleases
our friend the stranger to remain in,
I'll make you his guardians—
or if he wishes he may come with me.
Whatever you like, Oedipus: you can make your
     own choice   710
of what I offer and I'll accept it.

OEDIPUS May Zeus send blessings to such men!

THESEUS So what is your wish? To go to my home?

OEDIPUS If it were right. But *here* is the place.

THESEUS Where you'll do what? I'll not oppose it.

OEDIPUS Triumph over those who drove me out.

THESEUS It's a great thing, this gift?
Your being here with us?

OEDIPUS That depends on how you keep the bargain.

THESEUS Of me be certain: I'll not betray you.

OEDIPUS And I'll not bind you with an oath, like a coward.   720

THESEUS Even if you did, you'd get no more than when I
                    gave my word.

OEDIPUS But what will you do?

THESEUS What's your fear?

OEDIPUS Men will come—

THESEUS These men will deal with them.

OEDIPUS Beware, if you leave me—

THESEUS Don't teach me my duty.

OEDIPUS I can't help it. I'm afraid.

THESEUS In *my* heart there's no fear.

OEDIPUS You don't know the threats, the—   730

THESEUS What I know is that no one will take you
                    against my will. Even were they strong enough
                    to think of forcing you from here, I know they'll
                            soon see
                    how an ocean rolls between them and their deed
                    and there's no easy crossing. But even if
                    you pay no heed to my judgment, take heart—
                    if Phoebus indeed has led you here. And if I
                    am absent myself, no matter, for I know
                    my name alone is enough to protect you.

                              Exit THESEUS *in direction of Athens.*

CHORUS   Welcome stranger: in this country rich in horses   740
                you've come to the strongest dwellings in the world.
                Here is bright-shining white Colonus. Here
                the sweet-throated nightingale throngs with song
                glades the wind or sun won't touch.
                The wine-flecked ivy grows
                in these thick untrodden groves of the god.
                Fruit trees are free here from frigid winter
                and here with his immortal nurses roams the
                     roistering Dionysus.

                Bathed in the dew of the sky
                here the narcissus never withers—ever weaving an
                     ancient garland   750
                for the brows of the two Great Goddesses—and here
                     grows the golden crocus.
                Streams that flow here from the wide Cephisus
                never sleep and never empty:
                ever-running—never dry—day by day
                this pure water floods the plain
                and livens miles of fertile earth.
                Not even the Muses shun this place—nor golden-
                     reined Aphrodite.

                And something grows here
                that never grows—they say—in the fields of Asia
                or the famous Doric isle of Pelops: a tree seeding
                     itself by nature.   760
                Self-creating. Fearsome even
                to the weapons of our enemies:
                here the gray-leafed olive flourishes—nourisher
                     of children.
                Young or old—no man can lay a fatal hand on it
                for ever-waking Zeus protects it—patron
                of the Sacred Olive—and his gray-eyed child Athena.

                And here's one praise more for our mother city:
                it's this country's proudest boast—a present from the
                     god himself—

> god of horses colts and shining ocean.
> Son of Cronos: Lord Poseidon: it was you who raised
>   the city with this gift   770
> so we boast of it today. You gave us the
>   bridle-harness
> that heals horses of their wildness and on these
>   roads first transformed them.
> And you gave another wonder: oar-blades to tame
>   the waves
> and gallop flashing in the sea-nymphs' wake—
>   the Nereids
> on their hundred dancing feet.

A noise of many men arriving.

ANTIGONE O land praised with such high praises, now
          you'll have to make these words shine in deeds.

OEDIPUS   Child, what's happening?

ANTIGONE Creon, father, he's coming, and many with him.

OEDIPUS   Now, old men, dearest elders—this   780
          may test your safe-keeping to its limit.

Enter, from direction of Thebes, CREON *with soldiers.*

CHORUS LEADER Have courage, we'll keep you. For though I'm old,
               our country's strength has not grown old.

CREON   Men of this country, well-born natives:
        I clearly see in your eyes that you feel
        some fear at my coming among you. But
        you mustn't shrink from me or speak harsh words:
        I don't come like a man with big ambitions,
        since I'm old now and know I've come
        to a city as strong as any in Greece.   790
        But I've been sent, old as I am, to persuade this man
        to come to the land of the Cadmeians,

not just because one man demanded it,
but because all the citizens prompted me to it—
since, in the whole city, I and my family
grieved most for the sufferings of this man.
But wretched Oedipus, listen, and come home!
All the people of Thebes justly call you back,
and I more than any. For I, old man, am the one
who feels most deeply your afflictions—seeing
    you here   800
an unhappy exile, forever a beggar wandering
    without means
and depending on a girl I'd never have thought could
descend into such degradation (it grieves me to say it)
as she's fallen into, this unluckiest of girls: always
looking after you and the needs of your body;
poor, unmarried, a prey for any passing man.
And is this not a shocking reproach I've flung at you
in my distress, and at myself
and my whole family? But I may not hide
what's plain to see. So now, Oedipus, by the gods of
    our fathers   810
be persuaded by me: purge this shame.
Come willingly with me to the city of your birth;
follow me back to your father's house; give this city
a farewell blessing—she's earned it. But
you should show more respect to your native city,
which long ago gave you life.

OEDIPUS Oh you, you who'd stop at nothing,
twisting any just sentence into crooked sense.
Why try to lay hands on me a second time—
here like this, when I'd feel most grief?   820
Years ago, when I was stricken
with misfortunes that cut me to the quick—
so it would have been a joy to be cast out from my
    native place—
you were never willing to grant me this favor,
no matter how much I craved it. But when my
rage was spent at last, and I was glad to live
the rest of my days undisturbed in my own house,

then you wanted nothing but to cast me into exile
and drive me away. Then our kinship
meant nothing to you. But now, when you see
          this city   830
turn its face to me in friendship
and its citizens welcome me into their family,
now you try to draw me away from here, speaking
sour truths in your honeyed words. What good
is there in this? in this show of love
when it's not wanted? Just as if someone
would offer you nothing, no helping hand when you
          need it most,
but then, when your spirit is as full as you could wish,
only then would he give it, granting a useless favor.
Wouldn't this be a hollow pleasure? But this   840
is what you offer me—honorable words
and dishonorable deeds. But I'll proclaim you
to these men here, and let them see you
for the villain you are: You've come here
to take me away, but not to bring me home. You'll
          settle me
in some place nearby, keeping your city
free from harm, suffering nothing at the hands
          of Athens.
You'll not succeed in this. But I'll give you
something else: my vengeance
living forever in your country. And this   850
for my sons: they'll inherit just enough land
to stretch their bodies on in death.
Do I not understand what goes on in Thebes
better than you? Yes, much better,
because I hear more clearly than you
the words of Zeus and his son, Phoebus Apollo.
So here you are, with your traitor's mouth and
          brazen tongue!
But—though I can never convince you of this—
          your words
will only make trouble for you, not safe-keeping.
Go then, and leave us here to live our lives. Left
          to our   860

67

own will and pleasure, we won't live badly,
even as we're living now.

CREON   Do you think it's me you hurt with these words,
or will they wound your own wounded condition?

OEDIPUS My greatest pleasure will be your failure
to win over me or these men with me here.

CREON   Miserable man! Can't the years give you sense?
Are you just living to bring contempt on old age?

OEDIPUS You're good with your tongue, but I know
no good man
can contrive a just argument for every cause.   870

CREON   To speak a lot and speak to the point are
not the same.

OEDIPUS As if the little you say were to the point.

CREON   Not to someone with a mind like yours.

OEDIPUS Away! Go! Now I speak for these men too:
Don't stand in my way there like a guard
blockading the place where I'm to live.

CREON   I call on these men, not you, to witness
all you've said to me, your kinsman. If ever I
take you . . .

OEDIPUS Who could force me from these allies?

CREON   Even without that, I swear you'll suffer.   880

OEDIPUS What sort of threat is that?

CREON   Your two girls—I've seized one already
and sent her away. Now I'll take the other.

OEDIPUS   *With a loud moan.*
          Ohhh!

CREON   You'll soon have more than that to moan over.

OEDIPUS   You have my child?

CREON   I have, and in no time this one too.

OEDIPUS   Friends, what will you do? Will you betray me?
          Not drive this blasphemous man from your land?

CHORUS LEADER   Go, stranger! Away! Now!   890
          There's no justice in what you do,
          and none in what you've done already.

CREON   *To his men.*
          Now's the moment—*now!*—to bring this one away;
          if she doesn't come willingly, force her!

ANTIGONE   *With a shout of misery.*
          Aahhh! Where can I fly to? What help can I get
          from gods or from men?

CHORUS LEADER   What do you think you're doing, stranger?

CREON   I won't touch this man. But the girl is mine!

OEDIPUS   Lords of this land!

CHORUS LEADER   This isn't justice, stranger.   900

CREON   Yes, justice!

CHORUS LEADER   How justice?

CREON   I take what is mine!

OEDIPUS   *With a cry of horror.*
          Ohhh! *City!*

CHORUS   *Stranger! What are you doing?*
            Won't you release her?
            You'll meet—and soon—a test of strength.

CREON   *Back! Stay back!*

CHORUS   *Not from you—with these intentions.*

CREON   *Injure me and face my city in battle!*   910

OEDIPUS   *Isn't this what I told you?*

CHORUS   *Take your hands off her! Now!*

CREON   *Don't try giving orders where you have no power!*

CHORUS   *I say let go!*

CREON   *To his men.*
            And I say Go!

CHORUS   *Men of this land come quickly quickly!*
            Violent hands are laid on the city! My city!
            Come! Come quickly!

ANTIGONE   Strangers, friends, they're taking me away!

OEDIPUS   Where are you, child?   920

ANTIGONE   I'm being dragged away!

OEDIPUS   My child, reach me your hand.

ANTIGONE   I can't, I haven't the strength.

CREON   Take her away!

            The men drag ANTIGONE *off in the direction of Thebes.*

OEDIPUS   Oh wretched! *Wretched!*

CREON   You'll go no farther on these two crutches.
            But since you want to triumph over fatherland
                and friends,

whose orders, though I'm ruler, I carry out,
triumph away! In time I know you'll see the truth:
You're not doing yourself any good now,   930
and you haven't done any good in the past—the way
you oppose your friends, give free rein to your rage.
But it's yourself you make contemptible in the end.

CHORUS LEADER Hold, stranger!

CREON I tell you, don't touch me!

CHORUS LEADER If I don't get these girls back, I won't let you go.

CREON Then you'll soon pay my city a heavier fine!
I won't take only these women.

CHORUS LEADER What will you do?

CREON Seize this man and take him away with me.   940

CHORUS LEADER A terrible thing to say.

CREON And unless the ruler of this land prevents me,
this terrible thing will now be *done*.

OEDIPUS Shameless tongue! You say you'll lay hands on me?

CREON I say, *Be silent!*

OEDIPUS No! I will speak! May these divinities
yet permit me to utter this curse
on you, most craven of men, on you
who have violently taken this helpless girl
who is the only eyes I have: so you double the blow   950
struck years ago at my own two eyes. For this
may all-seeing Helios give you, and your kin,
a life like the life I've led in old age.

CREON Citizens, do you see this?

OEDIPUS Yes, they see you and me—me wounded by deeds,
            defending myself with words.

CREON Well then, I won't swallow my fury:
         Alone as I am, and slowed by age,
         I'll take this man by force!

OEDIPUS   *With a cry of despair.*
         Ohhh! *Misery!*   960

CHORUS *Stranger! What an insolent spirit you have*
         if you come here and think you'll do as you say.

CREON *I think so—yes.*

CHORUS *Then I count this city a city no longer.*

CREON *The weak man if his cause be just*
         still can overpower and cast down the strong.

OEDIPUS *You hear what he says?*

CHORUS *Zeus knows he won't bring this about.*

CREON *Zeus may know but you don't!*

CHORUS *Isn't this insolence?*   970

CREON *Yes insolence! And you have to take it!*

CHORUS *O people and chief men of the country:*
         these men are breaking bounds—crossing
            our borders!
         Come! Come running!

                        Enter THESEUS *from direction of Athens.*

THESEUS What's this cry? What's happening? What fear
            halted my sacrifice at the sea-god's altar, guardian
               of Colonus?
            Speak, so I'll know what there is to know.
            I've taxed my strength, hurrying here.

OEDIPUS Dearest lord—for I can tell it's you by your voice—
         how bitter my sufferings were just now   980
         at this man's hands.

THESEUS What sufferings? Who has hurt you? Speak.

OEDIPUS This one! Creon. You see him: he's going,
         and he's taken my only two children from me.

THESEUS What do you mean?

OEDIPUS That's what I've suffered.

THESEUS Let one of my men run to the altar
         with all speed. Tell all who are there
         to race from the sacrifice on horseback or on foot
         straight for the place where the two highways meet,   990
         so those girls may go no farther
         and I, bested by this brutish deed of his,
         not become a mockery to this stranger. So go,
         go quickly! Were I in a fury, as he deserves,
         he'd never escape unscathed. But now
         the laws, the laws he came here to uphold,
         will bring him to order.
                            You should know
         you'll not leave this country of ours
         till you bring these two girls back before me.
         You've acted in a manner unworthy of me, unworthy   1000
         of your ancestors and the land that bore you.
         You've come to a city that practices justice,
         where nothing is determined outside the law,
         yet you've wantonly flouted the authority
         of this country—bursting in like this
         and taking what you want, bringing your own
         force to bear. You think there are
         no men here or, if there are, you think
         they're slaves. And you think I'm nobody,
         I count for nothing. Yet Thebes   1010
         didn't bring you up to be bad: it's not her way
         to raise lawless men; she wouldn't condone

anything you've done, if she knew you'd
raided my property like this and
plundered what belongs to the gods, laying
violent hands on these two suppliants, these
wretched girls. Even with all the justification
    in the world,
I'd never cross over into your country
if I lacked permission from the rulers there.
And I'd never snatch away anyone or anything—   1020
because I know how a stranger should behave, always,
in a foreign city, among its citizens. But you,
you bring shame on a blameless city, you shame
your native place: the years have made you
both old and stupid. So, I've said it once
and I'll say it again: have someone
return these girls right away, unless you wish
to reside here by force against your will. In this
My thoughts and my words are one.

CHORUS LEADER   Now you see where you've got to, stranger: 1030
Coming from that city you seem a just man,
but your actions show you're a bad one.

CREON   I don't say, son of Aegeus, that your city
is lacking in manhood. And no bad counsel,
    as you say,
drove me to these actions. But I knew your people
would never feel such zeal for my relatives here
that they'd support them with violence
against me. And in my heart I knew
they'd never give shelter to a man
who murdered his own father. A polluted man,   1040
a man whose marriage—with all its intimacies—
was nothing but a sacrilege, the grossest offence.
And I knew your Council—that makes its home on
    Ares' hill—
was founded on order, and would never
permit vagrants like these to settle in the city.
Believing all this, I took hold of my prey—
and I'd never have done even that

had he not flung curses at me and my family.
What I suffered, I believe, made it just
for me to act as I've acted here.   1050
In face of all this, you may do as you wish,
since even if there's justice in what I say
I'm nothing in your eyes, being alone. But
old as I am, when the time is ripe
I'll strike whoever strikes me, blow for blow.

OEDIPUS Shameless arrogance! Whom do you think you wound
with these words? Me in my old age
or you in yours? You who've spewed out
murders and marriages and misfortunes, which I
in my wretchedness endured against my will. That   1060
was what pleased the gods—from some old
            anger, perhaps,
against my family. For if it were a question
of me alone, you couldn't with any justice
            reproach me
for any wrongdoing I paid for
by grievously wronging myself and mine.
So teach me, then: if a certain decree of the oracle
was hanging over my father's head, that said
he'd meet his death at the hands of his children,
how in justice blame me for this—I then
unfathered, unmothered, still unborn? And
            beyond that,   1070
if the light I was born to was the light of misery,
and I came to blows with my father and killed him—
knowing nothing of whom I fought, of what I did—
how could you blame me for an act
done in ignorance? And, wretch that you are,
you feel no shame in forcing me to speak—
as speak I will—of this marriage
to my mother, your own blood sister? You lack
all piety and let your tongue run away with you.
So yes, I'll speak now, I won't be silent: 1080
She gave birth to me, and she who bore me—*Aahh!*
the horror of it: I didn't know, she didn't know—
to her bitter shame conceived children with me.

Yet there's one thing I do know: that you
mouth these things willingly against me, against her,
while I, not willing it, wed her
and must speak of it now, though I've no wish to.
But I'll not hear myself called evil for this: neither
for the marriage nor for the murder—that
      bitter reproach
always in your mouth. Just answer me   1090
one question, it will settle everything:
if someone—anyone standing here this minute—
tried to kill you, you the just man, would you
stop to inquire if he was your father
or would you strike back to revenge the blow?
If you love your life, I think you'd quickly
repay in kind the one who struck first
and not look for the justice in it. And, with the gods
guiding me, that was exactly the trouble
that I walked into. So I think even my father's spirit,   1100
were he living, would have no reason
to argue against me. But you—you who are unjust
and think it right to say anything speakable or
      unspeakable—
you reproach me with such things in front of
      these men
and choose to flatter Theseus to his face, and
Athens too, praising her good order.
But though you're lavish in flattery
you forget this praise: that of all countries
this one knows best how to reverence the gods—
this land here from which you intended to   1110
snatch me away, an old man and a suppliant,
and tried to lay hands on me, and took my daughters.
To answer all this I call on the Goddesses,
and I beseech them and pray they will be my allies
and come to my aid, so you can learn
just what sort of men are guarding this city.

CHORUS LEADER My lord, this stranger is a good man.
We can see his misfortunes are calamitous,
but they deserve our protection.

THESEUS No more talk. At this moment the captors are
                    speeding away,   1120
                while we, the injured, stand still as stones.

   CREON Feeble as I am, what will you have me do?

THESEUS Lead the way to where these girls are. I alone
                will be your escort. I know
                you didn't come on your own or unprepared
                for the great violence and daring you've shown here.
                    You've relied
                on someone or something—which I must look to
                and not let the city be weaker than a single man.
                So lead me: if you're keeping these
                girls of ours, you can show me yourself.   1130
                But if their abductors have taken flight already
                we need do nothing: there are others
                racing ahead of us, from whom they'll never escape
                to give thanks to the gods. Lead on, then, and know
                that though you hold, you are held—
                you the hunter Fortune has trapped. For you see,
                things taken by unlawful deceit
                are never safe with those who take them.
                Do you understand this? Or does all I've said
                seem as useless as what *you* said   1140
                when you schemed and plotted to come here?

   CREON Since you're here, I can fault nothing you say to me.
                But, once home, we'll know what action to take.

THESEUS Threaten all you like—so long as you go. Now!

                    Exit CREON *and soldiers in direction of Thebes.*

                Oedipus, I ask you to stay here in peace for my sake.
                And trust that if I myself don't die
                I won't rest till I've restored your daughters.

OEDIPUS For this nobility may you prosper, Theseus:
for this even-handed care you show us.

Exit THESEUS *in direction of Thebes.*

CHORUS   *Would I could be where the men of war*   1150
will soon turn—turn and wade into
the brazen clash of the war-god's battle!
Either on Apollo's sandy shore
or the torchlit strand where the Great Goddesses
foster the rites of mortal creatures
whose tongues are sealed by the golden key of
the ministers there—children of Eumolpus.
Here I can see that battle-rouser Theseus
and these two captive virgin sisters
will come together at the sound of his war-shout—   1160
his sign of triumph.

On horseback in chariots I see them charging
in headlong flight from the pastures of Oea
to a place just west of the snow-white rocks.
He will be defeated!
Terrible the battle-rage of the men who live here—
terrible the might of Theseus's men.
Each bit and bridle flashes like lightning:
each rider gallops flat to the neck of his horse.
Horsemen who honor Athena of the horses.   1170
and that earth-encircling son of Rhea—
beloved son—god of the sea.

Do they press on? Do they pull back?
With trust now I beg that these two girls
who have endured dreadful discoveries
and suffered dread things at the hands of their kin—
that all their agonies may soon be over.
This day Zeus will accomplish something—
he'll accomplish something!
I am the prophet of this great contest: O
   that I could   1180

like a dove that is swift as the wind
soar to the clouds: see the strife from on high.

All-seeing Zeus! Overlord of the gods!
In this ambush may you open a path
for the men of this country to catch their prey—
victorious with powerful hands.
And may you Athena—revered daughter—
clear the way. And I pray
for the help of Apollo the hunter
and his sister who runs with the speckled fleet deer: 1190
may the two of them come
to aid this country and its citizens.

Friend, wandering man, you'll not say now
the watcher is a false prophet. For I see those
daughters again, your two girls, and they're in
          good company.

OEDIPUS Where? What are you saying? What do you mean?

          Enter, from the direction of Thebes, THESEUS *with*
                    ANTIGONE *and* ISMENE.

ANTIGONE Oh father, father! Which god might grant you
the gift of seeing this man—this best of men!—
who has brought us back to you?

OEDIPUS My child! Are the two of you here?   1200

ANTIGONE We are, father, we're here—because Theseus saved us
with his own good hands and those of his men.

OEDIPUS Come, child, come to your father. Come,
          let me touch
what I'd never hoped to touch again.

ANTIGONE You'll get your wish: for the gift we give
is what we long for.

OEDIPUS Where are you—the two of you?

ANTIGONE Here, together. Right beside you.

OEDIPUS Little ones, dearest green shoots!

ANTIGONE Dear to our father!   1210

OEDIPUS Props for a man—

ANTIGONE Ill-fated props for a man of misfortune.

OEDIPUS These dear ones, I hold them close.
         If I should die this very instant, I wouldn't
         be completely wretched, for these two
         are here beside me. Children, give me your support—
         one on each side—and take root
         in the man who planted you. Let both of you
         give him, abandoned till now, some rest from
         his straying and wandering.
                              And now   1220
         tell me what happened. Be as brief as you can:
         A short speech is always enough for younger women.

ANTIGONE Here's the man who saved us, father: it's him
         you must listen to; it was he who did it.
         So any speech of mine will be brief, as you say.

OEDIPUS My friend, don't be amazed that I insist on
         talking on like this with my children, who
         against all hope have come to light here.
         I know there's no cause except yourself
         for my fierce joy in these young ones of mine: 1230
         you made the light that shines on us here;
         it was you, no one else, who saved them.
         And may the gods provide for you as I'd wish,
         both you yourself and this your country.
         For only in you, all of you, have I found
         respect, right manners, and no false words.
         And now, with these words, I recognize

and repay your deeds. It's thanks to you and no other
that I have what I have.
Reach me your right hand, my lord,   1240
so I may, if it's proper, touch it and kiss you.
— But what am I saying? How could *I*, most wretched,
want *you* to touch a man
who wears the stain of every wrong? How could I
wish such a thing on you? No! I won't
let it happen! For none but those
who have lived through what I've lived through
can share what I've suffered. So receive
and return my greeting there where you stand,
and deal justly with me, as you've done this day.   1250

THESEUS   I'm not at all amazed, Oedipus,
that you've lingered over the joy you find
in feeling these two children beside you.
Nor do I think it strange you've seized
on their words before words of mine.
This doesn't trouble me at all. For it's
not with words that we wish to make life
luminous, but with our deeds. I myself, old man,
am proof of this. I've not broken a single word
of the oath I swore: these women here, I
          bring them back   1260
alive, unharmed, untouched by the danger
          they were in.
There's no need to boast with empty words
how we won this hard-fought battle; you'll learn
          all about it
in the company of these two daughters. But here's
          a report now
come to my hands by chance as I hurried back:
tell me what you think of it. In words it's brief,
but still surprising. And a man should never
          take lightly
anything that happens.

OEDIPUS   What is it, son of Aegeus? Tell me.
I know nothing of what you're asking.   1270

81

THESEUS They say that some man, some kin of yours but not a
                fellow-citizen,
            came running out of nowhere
            and is this minute sitting at that altar of Poseidon
            where I was sacrificing before I set out.

OEDIPUS Where is he from? What does he hope for, taking
                that seat?

THESEUS This is all I know: they tell me
            he only wants a short talk with you, and no
                trouble in it.

OEDIPUS What sort of talk? His sitting like that, there
            at the altar—it must be something of importance.

THESEUS They say he just wants to talk with you face to face   1280
            and then go away, unharmed by his coming.

OEDIPUS Who could he be, come to the altar like this?

THESEUS Think—have you any kinsman in Argos
            who might want a favor like this from you?

OEDIPUS My dear friend, stop where you are!

THESEUS What is it?

OEDIPUS Do not ask it of me.

THESEUS Ask what? Tell me.

OEDIPUS From your words I can tell exactly who it is
            there like that, supplicating the gods.   1290

THESEUS Who, then? Who is this man I might find fault with?

OEDIPUS My son! It's my son, my lord. I despise him.
His words would cause me more pain
than those of any other man.

THESEUS Why? Is it not possible simply to listen
and not do anything you don't wish to do?
Why is it so painful to hear him out?

OEDIPUS This voice, my lord, is the most loathed voice
that could ever find its way to a father's ear.
Don't force me to yield in this.   1300

THESEUS But if his sitting in supplication asks it of you?
Mustn't you remember your respect for the god?

ANTIGONE Father, I'm young, a woman, but listen to me:
let Theseus give to his own heart and to the god
the satisfaction of what he wishes. And for
          our sakes, too,
let this brother come. For if what he says
will do you no good, you can be sure
it won't drag you from the path you've chosen.
What harm, then, to listen to words? Speech
can bring to light evil intentions. Even if he did you   1310
most grievous wrong, it wouldn't be right
to give ill for ill: he is your child; show him
some understanding. Other men have bad children
and feel deep anger; but rebuked
by the gentle appeals of those dear to them,
they soften their hearts. You, you especially,
don't look to the present,
but consider those pains you yourself suffered
because of your father and your mother.
If you look at them, I know you'll see   1320
how a bad intent in turn ends in bad. Undeniable
the reminders you have of this,
deprived as you are of your two eyes.
So let us have our way, give us what we ask.
It isn't good to have to beg for what's right—

for a man who has been treated kindly
not to know how to answer in kind.

OEDIPUS   Your words, child, have won a heavy pleasure.
So since you want it so much, let it be.

To THESEUS.

Only, my friend, if that man is to come here,   1330
you mustn't let anyone take charge of my life.

THESEUS   Only once, old man, do I need to hear
the words you've spoken. I've no wish to boast,
but know you are safe, if a god keeps me so.

Exit THESEUS, *in direction of Athens.*

CHORUS   *For me the man*
              who wants more life than his measured lot
              will be revealed in the end for all to see
              shielding a life bent out of shape.
              For the long days hold in store
              many things to steer us nearer to pain   1340
              and it's in vain we look for pleasure
              in a life spun out past its given span.
              And when Hades comes to play his part
              helping all to the one end
              no wedding-songs then no lyre no dancing
              only death at the end of all.

              Never to be born is the best story.
              But when one has come to the light of day
              second-best is to leave and go back
              quick as you can back where you came from.   1350
              For in his giddy light-headed youth
              what sharp blow isn't far from a man? What
                 affliction—
              strife death dissension the ache of envy—
              isn't close by? And in the end
              his lot is to lack all power:
              despised and cast out in friendless old age

where a man lives with nothing
but one hardship topping another.

I'm not alone in this: this wretch here—
as a northern shore lashed by sea and storm   1360
is battered flat from every side
so wave after wave of ruin and destruction
batter at this wretched man.
And they keep on coming:
from the place of the setting sun and its rising—
from the bright mid-point of day they come
and the bleak northern peaks of midnight.

ANTIGONE And here's the stranger, father, or so it seems.
He's alone at least, and as he makes his way toward us
his two eyes overflow with tears.   1370

OEDIPUS Who is it?

       Enter, from the direction of Athens, POLYNEICES.

ANTIGONE The man we've had all this while in our thoughts:
Polyneices. He's here.

POLYNEICES   *With a moan.*
Ohhh! What am I to do? Should I weep, sisters,
first, for my own sorrows or, seeing his sufferings,
let my tears fall
for this old man, my father, whom I find
here with the two of you, banished
to this place of strangers? Dressed in filthy
old rags that have rotted his flesh;   1380
and the matted hair of his head—his eyeless head!—
tangled by every breeze; and his pouch
no different, the one he carries
for food scraps to fill his miserable belly.
To my shame I've come too late
to see all this. But now I myself
bear witness against myself: in caring for you

I've been the worst of men; there's no need to
    hear this
from another's tongue. But since Compassion
shares the throne with Zeus in all he does,   1390
let her stand beside you also, father—
for the wrongs that are done have some cure
and they're over now, there'll be no more of them.
Why are you silent?
Make some sound, father, don't turn your back
    on me.
Can you not offer a single word? Will you
treat me with contempt? Will you send me away
in silence again, with no explanation
even for your rage?
                Daughters of this man, sisters
of my blood: try to liven his mouth   1400
that's silent as a stone, there's no moving it. .
I beg you: don't let him spurn me like this—
while I stand a suppliant, at least to the god.
Not one answering word?

ANTIGONE Unhappy man: tell him yourself why you've come.
    Sometimes
words can draw a voice from silence, either for
some pleasure they bring, or by prompting
those who hear them to anger or pity.

POLYNEICES That's good advice: I'll speak out. But first
I call on the god to help me, from whose shrine   1410
the lord of this land led me, and gave me leave
to speak and listen, and to have safe passage
away from here. And strangers, I'd have this
from you too, and the promise of it
from my father and sisters.
                Now, father,
I want to tell you what I've come for:
I've been driven from my native land into exile
because I claimed the right, as the eldest born,
to sit on your throne and be sole ruler. Eteocles then,

though younger, answered by driving me out
    of the country.   1420
He defeated me not in any test of words or
    feat of arms
but by winning the city to his side. And I'm sure
that lurking behind all this is the Fury
who pursues you. Then, when I'd gone to Doric Argos
and taken Lord Adrastos there as my father-in-law,
I made sworn allies of all the chief men
among the Peloponnesian people—honored
    warriors all.
With their help I gathered against Thebes
a great force spearheaded by seven captains,
so I'd either perish there in a just battle   1430
or drive out of that land
those who have done these wicked deeds.
Let that be. But now, why am I here? Full
of suppliant prayers I've come to you, father—
my own prayers and those of my allies, camped now
with their seven spears and seven armies
across the great plain of Thebes. Men like
spear-shaking Amphiareus, first among warriors
and first too for reading signs
in the flight of birds. Second, the Aitolian son   1440
of Oineus, Tydeus he's called. Third,
Eteoclos, by birth an Argive. Hippomedon
is fourth, sent by his father, Telaos.
Fifth among them is Capaneus, who boasts
how he'll ravage the city of Thebes with fire
and fling it to destruction. Sixth
is an Arcadian, Parthenopaeus, who surges to battle
bearing a name that honors the virgin Atalanta,
she who in time became his mother; he
is her trusted son. And I, your son—   1450
or if not your son then a man conceived by
some awful destiny and deemed yours—
I lead this fearless army of Argives
against Thebes. These, father, all of us,
now beg you—as you value these children

and your own life—to let go
the fierce anger you feel against me,
as I march out now to repay my brother
who cast me away with nothing, stripped me
of my fatherland. Because—if we're to believe
    the oracles—   1460
the power lies with those who have you
as their ally. So now I implore you, by the
clear springs and the gods of our family—be
persuaded: give in to my words. Because we
are exiles and beggars, you are a stranger,
and we survive by fawning on others, the two of us
who have the one destiny. But—the thought
sickens me!—he who remains sole ruler
in our house, and lives in luxury, mocks
both of us in the same way. But I'll smash him   1470
into little pieces with ease
if you're my ally and think as I do.
And once I've driven him out,
I'll bring you home and settle you in your house,
and settle myself there too. But I can
make such a boast only if you join
your will to mine, for without you I know
I won't even have the strength to come back alive.

CHORUS LEADER Oedipus, for the sake of the one who sent him,
            tell the man what you think is right,   1480
            then send him on his way.

OEDIPUS Well then, you men who live here and guard
              this land—
        if Theseus hadn't sent this man to me
judging it right that he receive my answer,
he'd never hear the sound of my voice. But now
since he's been deemed worthy, he'll go away
having heard things which won't bring his life
much joy.
            Most vicious of men! When
you held scepter and throne in the city of Thebes
where your brother now rules alone, it was you   1490

who drove your own father away, making him
stateless, a homeless man. And you put
these clothes on him, which now you see and
now you weep at, now you've been caught out
in the same storm of sufferings as myself. But this
isn't something to spill a few tears over:
this has to be endured, endured by me
as long as I live, and with the memory of you
as my destroyer. It was you who gave me
this bitter bread. You who cast me out. Because
          of you   1500
I wander from day to day a beggar, begging
what I need to get through each day.
If I hadn't conceived these girls, these children
who take care of me, I'd not be alive at all,
for all the good *you've* done me. As it is,
these women keep me alive: they nurse
all my needs—these women
who are men, not women at all, in the way
they've shared the troubles I've had. But you
and your brother! The pair of you   1510
are sons of some other man, not mine. So
now your destiny gazes at you, but it does not
stare you straight in the face—as it will very soon
if those gathered armies march on Thebes.
For there's not the smallest chance in the world
you'll destroy that city. Before that happens,
you and your brother will fall in battle—fall
and lie stained and polluted in your own blood.
Such are the curses I once laid on you, and now
I summon these same curses to come   1520
as my ally, so you may think it worthwhile
to respect those who conceived you, and so
you may not escape the dishonor of behaving
as you've behaved to a sightless father. These girls
never did such things! So these curses of mine—
they smother your supplication, and your throne too,
if Justice herself, ancient in name,
shares by ancient law the seat of Zeus.
Away! I spit you out! I disown you! You

are worst of the wicked! Take   1530
these curses I call down on you:
Never to conquer your native land
with the spear of victory! Never
to get home safe to the plains of Argos,
but to kill, and die with, him who expelled you!
This is my curse, and I call on Tartarus,
the hateful, all-fathering dark itself, to take you
to another home! And I call on these Goddesses
and Ares himself—that god of war
who has driven the two of you to terrible hate!   1540
So hear this, and go. Go tell the Argives and your
        trusted allies
that Oedipus has given his own sons
such gifts as these, such honors!

CHORUS LEADER Polyneices, I take no pleasure in your journey here.
So go, quickly, back where you came from.

POLYNEICES   *Groaning.*
Aahhh! Such a journey it's been! And to fail like this!
Ohhh! I grieve for my comrades: what an end
to the march from Argos we all rallied for.
To come to such an end sickens my heart.
Ohhh! And I can speak of it   1550
to none of my companions, nor can I shy from it,
but must meet in silence whatever happens.
Sisters, you who share this man's blood with me:
Since you hear my father fling bitter curses,
you—you at least—if the curses of our father
        bear fruit,
and you get back to your home in Thebes,
do not revile and dishonor me
but bury me yourselves with funeral offerings,
so the praise you now win from our father
for all the hard ways you take care of him   1560
will have one more praise added, just as true,
because of what you'll do for me.

ANTIGONE Polyneices, I beg you, please, listen to me!

POLYNEICES   What is it, dearest Antigone? Tell me.

ANTIGONE   Turn your army; lead it back to Argos. Right away.
Don't destroy yourself and that city.

POLYNEICES   I can't.
How could I lead the same force there again,
if I'd shown them, even once, that I was afraid?

ANTIGONE   But why there again? Why such anger? What good is
it to you   1570
to destroy your country?

POLYNEICES   It's shameful for me to run away. Shameful
for me the elder to be mocked by my brother.

ANTIGONE   Don't you see then how you fulfill
the prophecies of this man here
who bellows death on both of you at each
other's hands?

POLYNEICES   Yes, that's what he wants. Mustn't we go along
with it?

ANTIGONE   *With a groan of misery.*
Aahhh! Who will follow you
when he hears the doom our father predicted?

POLYNEICES   But I won't report the darker details.   1580
The role of any true leader
is to give only good news, nothing less.

ANTIGONE   That's your decision?

POLYNEICES   It is; don't stop me. But for myself, this journey
must now be all my thought. Thanks
to my father and his Furies it's doomed
and bound for disaster. But may Zeus grant
the two of you
his favor, if you do what I've asked.

Let me go now. Farewell. You'll never see me again
while I'm alive to see you.   1590

ANTIGONE   *With a keening cry.*
    Ohh! Ohh! Ohh!

POLYNEICES No, don't weep for me.

ANTIGONE But brother, who would not weep for you,
    seeing you rush open-eyed toward Hades?

POLYNEICES If it must be, then I'll die.

ANTIGONE Don't die! Listen to me!

POLYNEICES Don't argue me into what must not be.

ANTIGONE My heart is broken then, if I'm to lose you.

POLYNEICES Whether things go one way or the other
    is in the hands of the god. But I pray   1600
    that you two meet no disaster. The world knows
    you don't deserve misfortune.

                    Exit POLYNEICES *in direction of Thebes.*

CHORUS   *From some new source*
          I see strange things coming:
          horrors heavy with death from the sightless stranger
          or destiny itself reaching its end here.
          For I can say whatever the gods think worthwhile
          will never come to nothing. Time
          holds all things always in its eye:
          some it pitches down   1610
          and next day raises others from the dust.
                                        Sound of thunder.
          Thunder in the air! Ah Zeus!

OEDIPUS Children! Children! If there's anyone here,
    send them for Theseus, that peerless man!

ANTIGONE Why do you summon him, father? For what
                        good purpose?

OEDIPUS Soon Zeus's thunderbolt will take me to Hades.
                But send for him, quickly!

Sound of thunder.

CHORUS   *Again! Look! Huge the flashing crash of it!*
                  Clamor unspeakable! This hurled bolt!
                  Fear slithers to the roots of my hair: 1620
                  like a frighted creature my spirit is shivering.
                  Lightning sets fire to the heavens again!
                  What end will he unleash upon us?
                  I fear it. For lightning never flashes to no purpose—
                  never without some misfortune or other.
                  Oh! Endless sky! Ah! Zeus!

OEDIPUS It's come, children: the end of my life as the
                        gods foretold.
                And now there's no turning it away.

ANTIGONE How do you know? What sign makes you think so?

OEDIPUS I know it well. But for my sake now   1630
                send someone to the lord of this land
                and bring him to me.

Sound of thunder.

CHORUS   *With a cry of terror.*
                  Aaahhh! See! Again!
                  All around us ear-splitting din!
                  Mercy mighty power show mercy!
                  Mercy if you're bringing down some
                  dark invisible thing to mother earth!
                  Let me find you just
                  and not—because I've looked at a man accursed—
                  reap a reward that has no good in it.   1640
                  To you I cry—Lord Zeus!

OEDIPUS Children, is he coming yet? Will he find me
        still alive and in my right mind?

ANTIGONE What is it you want to keep your mind clear for?

OEDIPUS To give them, as I promised, a fulfilling favor,
        in return for the good I got from them.

Sound of thunder.

CHORUS   With a pleading cry.
        Ohh! Ohh! *Come! Come my son!*
        Even if you're sacrificing to Poseidon
        —making his high hearth holy with the blood
          of cattle—
        come to us here! For this stranger   1650
        thinks you your friends and this our city
        worth honoring with fair recompense
        for all the favor he's had here. Oh
        come Lord! Hurry! Come! Come running!

Enter THESEUS, *from direction of Athens.*

THESEUS What's this uproar?
        I can hear your voices in it and the voice of
          the stranger.
        Because of Zeus's own thunderbolt, is it?
        Or his hailstones hammering down? It's possible
        to imagine anything when a god comes storming.

OEDIPUS My lord, you've come as I've wished! Some god   1660
        has given your journey a fortunate end.

THESEUS What's happened, son of Laius?

OEDIPUS My life's balance is dipping. I don't want to die
        false to my promise to you and your city.

THESEUS What tells you you're about to die?

OEDIPUS The gods themselves tell me.
         Not one of the promised signs was false.

THESEUS How are these things made clear, old man?

OEDIPUS By divine thunder rolling over and over,
         bolt after flaming bolt from an almighty hand.   1670

THESEUS I believe you, for I see you've foretold much
         and not spoken falsely. Tell me what I must do.

OEDIPUS I will teach you, son of Aegeus, things
         which age can never spoil, things that now
         will lie in store for this city. And soon,
         without the touch of any guide, I'll take you
         to the place where I shall die. Don't ever
         show this place to anyone: keep the region secret,
         along with the ground where this burial-site
         lies hidden. So year after year this spot may be   1680
         a defense mightier than a multitude of shields,
         stronger than the spears of neighboring mercenaries.
         And the sacred things I cannot speak of, when you go
         alone to that place, you'll understand them: for I may
         not reveal them to any of these citizens, nor even
         to my own daughters, however much I love them.
         So be sure to keep them safe always,
         and when the time comes for you to die
         give these signs to the chief man among you,
         and let him reveal them to his successor,   1690
         and so let it go on forever. That way
         you will live in an unscathed city
         which the dragon-seed men will never ravage.
         For countless cities—however well ordered
              some may be—
         turn easily to violence. But no matter how late,
         the clear-sighted gods see when someone
         turns away from them and embraces madness.
         Son of Aegeus, don't ever wish
         to experience this. But I teach such things

to one who knows them already. Let us go, then: 1700
for this sign from the god now urges me
on to that place: let nothing any longer hold us back.
Children,

                                               He rises.

follow me. For, strange as it seems,
now it is I who am your guide, just as you
have always guided your father. Come.

                      He slowly moves towards the grove.

And lay no hand on me. Let me be.
Let me discover all on my own
the blessed tomb where it is my lot
to be hidden away in the earth at last.   1710
This way, come. Come this way. This is the way
the guide Hermes leads me, and the Goddess
who dwells below. O light invisible! Once, somehow,
you belonged to me. But now my body
feels your touch for the last time: I go now
to hide my life, at its end, in sightless Hades.
But you, dear man, dearest of strangers,
may you yourself, this land, and your people
flourish and prosper. And when I'm dead,
in your well-being remember me.   1720
And may good fortune be with you forever.

           He moves purposefully into the grove, THESEUS,
               ISMENE, ANTIGONE *others following.*

CHORUS   *If it's right for me to show reverence with prayers*
        to the unseen Goddess and to you—
        master of those who dwell in darkness: Aidoneus!
          Aidoneus!—
        I pray that the stranger may without pain
        without a death that draws deep lamentation
        reach the plains of the dead that hide everything
        and the house of Styx.
        For though he's suffered greatly and to no purpose
        a just power may exalt him again.   1730

                               Peal of thunder.

> O Goddesses of earth! And you
> invincible creature who lie down to sleep
> before those gates which greet many strangers—you
> who whimper before that cave—indomitable
> guard they say at the entrance to Hades—
> I beseech this son of Earth and Tartarus
> to make a safe passage for the stranger
> as he hurries headlong
> toward Hades and the plains of the dead.
> You I call on—Lord of endless sleep!   1740

Enter MESSENGER *from the direction of Athens.*

MESSENGER   Men of the city! The quickest way I could tell
>   my story
would be to say, "Oedipus is dead!" But no
>   short speech
could explain what happened, nor even
could the deeds themselves, many as they were.

CHORUS LEADER   Then he's dead, the unfortunate man?

MESSENGER   Know this for sure: he's left this daily life of ours.

CHORUS LEADER   Unhappy man! How did it happen?
Was his end painless? Was it god-ordained?

MESSENGER   Indeed it was, which makes the wonder of it.
You were here, and you know already   1750
how he went forward from this place
with none of his dear ones guiding him, but
>   he himself
guiding us all. But then, when he neared
the threshold there—steep as a cliff, with its great
bronze steps rooted in the earth—then he stood still
on one path where the path divides, just there
where a stone bowl marks the pact, everlasting,
between Theseus and Peirithous. And there—
halfway between that and Thoricos Rock, between
the hollow pear tree and the tomb of stone—   1760

97

he sat down. Then, unwinding his filthy rags, those
clothes he wore, he shouted orders to his children
to bring water from the near stream
for washing and making a libation.
So right away the two of them ran
to Demeter's stony rise, which stood in full view—
Demeter, mother of all young plants. Then,
with no more delay they brought him back
all he asked for, preparing him, as the custom is,
by bathing him and changing his garments.   1770
Then, when he'd done all he wished to do
and every one of his desires was met,
earth-dwelling Zeus thundered out
and the two young women shuddered at the sound
and fell at their father's knee in tears
and kept beating their breasts and wouldn't give up
their loud wailing cries. But he,
when he heard their sudden bitter cries,
folded them both in his arms, and he said:
Children, on this day you have no father.   1780
All that was my life is destroyed on me now:
you won't ever again have to labor for me
or look after me as you've always done.
I know, children, what a hard life it's been.
But there's one thing can dispel it all,
one word is enough to wipe hardship away:
Love, that this man had for you—no man
can love you more. And now the two of you
must go on living the rest of your lives
without him. So he spoke, and the three of them
          together   1790
embraced each other, sobbing and crying.
But when they'd shed their last tear at last
and no more loud cries were filling the air,
then there was silence.
                    Then, all of a sudden,
a voice, some voice, someone
was summoning him. And every one of us
felt the hair stand up on our heads with fear.
For again and again a god calls him,

echoing from every direction at once:
You! You there! Oedipus! Why   1800
do we put off our departure like this? What
a long delay you're making! Then,
when he heard himself called by the god,
he asked that Theseus, lord of this land, should
   draw near.
And when Theseus had approached, he said:
Friend of my heart, give these children
the pledge of your hand, that time-honored pledge.
And you, children, give your hands to this man.
Promise me you'll never give up these women
willingly to anyone. Promise me   1810
you'll always do what your heart tells you
is for their good. Then Theseus, that
   large-hearted man,
without pity or tears promised under oath
that for the stranger he'd do all he was asked.
And when all this was finished, Oedipus
laid both his blind hands on his two children:
Children, he said, *you must be brave now,*
and go away from this place,
and not judge it right to see what's forbidden
or hear men say what must not be heard.   1820
So go now. Go quickly away.
Let Theseus alone, who has authority here, remain
to learn the things that are done in this place.
All of us there, we heard him say this,
and with those two young women — in tears,
with loud moans — we moved away. But soon
we turned, and from far off
we saw that man was nowhere to be seen,
and the king himself was holding his hand up
to shade his eyes, as if there appeared some   1830
awesome terror, and he couldn't bear the sight.
Then, in a little while, we see him, in silence,
making a grave and stately bow
at once to the earth and Olympus of the gods.
But what sort of death took that man's life
no mortal tongue could tell, except

Theseus himself, that dear lord. No flaming
thunderbolt from god dispatched him,
and he wasn't snatched by a sudden sea-squall—
but it was either some escort from the gods in heaven   1840
or those below in the land of the dead,
or the dark deep earth itself breaking open
with kindness. For the man was taken
with no groaning, nor the pain of any sickness
        on him:
his death a wonder, surely, if any man's death is.
All I've spoken may seem mad to you,
but I make no apology nor seek to be excused
by anyone here who thinks me mad indeed.

CHORUS LEADER   Where are his children?
And the friends who went with them?   1850

MESSENGER   The girls aren't far off.

                                    Sound of keening.
There, that's the sound of their crying: they're close at
        hand.

                    Enter ANTIGONE *and* ISMENE *from the direction
                                            of Athens.*

ANTIGONE   *With a wail of despair.*
        Aaahhh! For us it is for us indeed
        two ill-fated women to bewail
        not once or twice but forever and ever
        the indelibly cursed blood of a father
        filling our veins!
        Once his life was a hardship to us
        a heavy everlasting trouble—
        but now at the end we'll carry away   1860
        things we can't account for at all
        although we've seen and suffered them.

CHORUS   *What? What has happened?*

ANTIGONE   *Friends—you can guess.*

CHORUS   *He's gone?*

ANTIGONE   *Gone—and just as you'd hope:*
              For how could you ever think otherwise
              and he not taken by Ares or the surging sea
              but snatched off to the Invisible Fields.
                  Carried away
              by a death that's secret and strange.   1870
              Poor sister!
              Death-dealing night has settled on our eyes!
              Wandering in a far-off land
              or over the waves of some distant sea
              how shall we weather this hard life at all?

ISMENE   *I don't know. May fatal Hades take me*
              down to my father: to die
              in my misery with him old as he was—
              for the life to come isn't worth living.

CHORUS   *Best pair of children:*   1880
              Try to bear bravely what the god gives.
              Don't let the blaze of these feelings inflame you.
              There's nothing to blame in what you've come to.

ANTIGONE   *But one can even long to have hardship back:*
              for what's not dear was dear to me
              when I held him in these two arms.
              Oh father! Dear father! You who now
              wear darkness under the earth forever: even there
              you'll never lose her love or mine.

CHORUS   *He fared—*   1890

ANTIGONE   *As he wished.*

CHORUS   *What do you mean?*

ANTIGONE   *Dying in the foreign land he longed for*
              and now he has his bed
              below in the kindly shade forever
              and the grief he left behind finds tears.
              For father I grieve for you indeed—these eyes

overflow with tears—and sorrowstruck I don't
    know how
to make such grief go away.

                                    With a groan.

Ohhh!   1900
Your wish was to die in a foreign land
but you died like this—
far from me. All alone.

ISMENE   With a keening cry.

Ohhh! And what fate
waits for me a wretched girl
or dear sister waits for you
now our father has deserted us?

CHORUS   *But since at last*
he was content to let his life go—
dear girls cease grieving: 1910
misfortune easily seizes men.

ANTIGONE   *Sister let's fly back—*

ISMENE   *To do what?*

ANTIGONE   *I'm caught by a wild desire.*

ISMENE   *What desire?*

ANTIGONE   *To see the home there in the earth—*

ISMENE   *Whose home?*

ANTIGONE   *My heart is broken! Our father's home!*

ISMENE   *But how could it be right? Don't you see that?*   1920

ANTIGONE   *Why do you rebuke me?*

ISMENE   *And this too—*

ANTIGONE   *Again! What is it?*

ISMENE   *That he fell*
far from everyone.
There is no tomb!

ANTIGONE   *Take me there—*
             then kill me too!

ISMENE   With a wail of despair.
             Aaahhh!
             Wretched life! How will I live?   1930
             Abandoned again! Helpless! Poor!

CHORUS   *Dear girls have no fear.*

ANTIGONE   *But where can I escape to?*

CHORUS   *You both escaped before.*

ANTIGONE   *What?*

CHORUS   *You fell into no harm.*

ANTIGONE   *Yet I'm thinking—*

CHORUS   *What are you thinking?*

ANTIGONE   *We can't get home.*

CHORUS   *Don't try.*   1940

ANTIGONE   *Trouble holds us hard.*

CHORUS   *That was so before.*

ANTIGONE   *Hard then. Impossible now.*

CHORUS   *A sea of troubles has been your lot.*

ANTIGONE   *Yes! Yes!*

CHORUS   *That's what I say too.*

ANTIGONE   With a gasp of despairing resignation.
             Aaahhh! Zeus! Where can we go?
             Toward what hope now
             will the god-force drive me?

                              Enter THESEUS *from the grove.*

THESEUS   Girls, cease your lamentations, wipe away your tears.   1950
          For when earth's darkness is given to one as a gift,
               a grace,
          let there be no grieving: it tempts the gods' anger.

ANTIGONE Son of Aegeus, we fall at your knees.

THESEUS For what, my children? What can I give you?

ANTIGONE With our own eyes
we would see the place where our father is buried.

THESEUS But it isn't lawful or right to go there.

ANTIGONE Lord of Athens, what do you mean?

THESEUS He forbade me this very thing, children,
that anyone should ever go near that place   1960
or break the silence of that blessed sanctuary
where he abides. And he told me
if I followed his words I'd keep this country forever
free of suffering and harm. And the god
heard us, and so did Oath, Zeus's son
who hears all we say.

ANTIGONE If this indeed was his final wish, we must be satisfied.
But send us back now to Thebes, land of
our ancestors:
we may yet, somehow,
stop the slaughter rushing toward our brothers.   1970

THESEUS I'll do that, and whatever else would in any way
serve you,
and please him who has gone just now
under earth's lid. I must be always ready for this,
and never grow weary.

CHORUS LEADER But cease now, cease your keening:
for in every way these things stand under
the steady sway of some shaping power.

NOTES ON THE TEXT

The numbers in bold refer to the line numbers in the translation; they are followed by the line numbers in the Greek text of the play edited by H. Lloyd-Jones and N. Wilson and published by Oxford University Press (1990; hereafter Oxford Classical Text, or OCT).

1–134 / 1–116 Prologue: In this section of the play before the entrance of the chorus, Sophocles establishes the physical setting and introduces the question: where does Oedipus belong?

47–48 / 43 *In other places they rightly have other names* The Eumenides are also referred to as Furies, Erinyes, the Dread Ladies, Holy Ones, or Implacable Maidens.

65 / 57 It is possible that the *Bronze-footed Threshold* marked an entrance to the underworld.

135–269 / 117–253 Parodos: the entrance-song of the chorus. The chorus enters from the direction of Athens. They are elderly citizens of Colonus who have heard that someone has entered the grove of the Furies, and they have come to protect the grove and themselves from this transgression. Choruses in Greek tragedy, made up of a group of fifteen men who sing and dance in the orchestra (the circular space in the theater between the semi-circular seating for the audience and the stage and skene) are the oldest element in the evolutionary growth of the genre. We know little about the choreography of their dance, but the words of their songs reveal to us the rhythms to which they danced. Very often their opening song or chant is set to an anapaestic rhythm—short beat, short beat, long beat—to which it is easy to process slowly onto the stage. In this case the chorus comes hurrying in to a livelier rhythmical pattern because they have heard the news of a stranger's intrusion into the grove. Choral songs create, by the difference in the way they are performed and in what they say, a contrast with the episodes, or conversations among actors. Although the chorus is given a group character appropriate to the action of the play, it is never fully immersed in the action of the play. Aeschylus, Sophocles, and Euripides use their choruses differently not only from each other but often from play to play. In this play the contrast between choral songs and episodes is somewhat modified by Sophocles' frequent use of the *kommos*, or sung exchange between chorus and an actor or actors, in place of the choral song. For example, after line 150 (137) Oedipus joins the chorus's song, first chanting anapaests with them and then at line 186 (179) sharing their song, as does Antigone at line 191 (182).

270–739 / 254–667 1st Episode: The episode falls into two parts, divided by a *kommos* between Oedipus and the chorus (553–608 /510–48). In the first part Oedipus' daughter/sister Ismene arrives from Thebes to give Oedipus news of recent oracles concerning him; in the second part Theseus enters, in response to Oedipus' request, and offers Oedipus a home in Athens.

292–93 / 274 *but those at whose hands I suffered / I was knowingly destroyed by them.* Oedipus here refers to Jocasta's and Laius' decision to leave him exposed in the wild as an infant, with his ankles pierced, because they had received a prophesy that he was destined to kill his father.

295 / 275 Supplication was a ritual act that often had serious consequences for both those who supplicated and those who received the suppliant; a number of Greek tragedies dramatize those consequences. If someone in need made himself or herself a suppliant to another with the power to help, both parties were bound by rules of behavior that the Greeks believed were enforced by Zeus Hikesios (Zeus of the Suppliants).

371ff. / 337ff. Oedipus' reference to "Egyptian habits" reflects an assumption common to many Greeks that Egyptian culture was a mirror image of their own, substituting "normal" practices with their opposites. However, educated Greeks (such as the historian Herodotos) also had a deep respect for Egyptian culture, recognizing it as older than their own and having had a deep influence on it.

387 / 354 *with all those prophecies* These earlier prophecies gave Oedipus the knowledge he refers to in his earlier conversation with the Stranger, that he

would find his final resting place in the grove of the Eumenides and that his presence would constitute a gift to those who received him in their land.

402–3 / 367–69 Creon, Oedipus' uncle and brother-in-law and Jocasta's brother, became king after Oedipus discovered that his patricide and incest were the cause of the plague destroying Thebes and consequently blinded himself. Oedipus' family is descended from Cadmus, the founder of Thebes. The myth of this family, like many mythical families, includes several instances of violence committed against family members by family members in a struggle for power.

438–39 / 401–2 The prophecies seem to indicate that whoever protects and controls Oedipus' tomb will receive protection from it. The Thebans cannot bury Oedipus within their walls, because he killed his father, but they can hope to watch over the tomb and receive its protection, if he is brought back to Thebes and, when he dies, is buried just outside the walls.

506ff. / 466ff. The description that follows gives us a very immediate sense of how a purification ritual was performed. Sophocles' inclusion of such a full description marks the importance he gives in the play to the laws by which humans order their lives and also to their limits. For example, the careful description of this ritual makes it clear that it belongs to a particular place and group of people; it is the kind of thing Oedipus must learn anew each time he comes to a new place. Yet Oedipus seems to invest it with a meaning that transcends its local practice (for further discussion, see the Introduction, pp. 10, 13).

569 / 521ff. The manuscript here reads "I bore it unwillingly or unknowingly," but there must be a corruption in the text because the manuscript reading is metrically impossible. We follow the Oxford Classical Text's (OCT) reading "willingly" (accepted by many other editors) and assume that Oedipus is here making a reference both to his self-blinding and his acceptance of exile.

572 / 525 Oedipus refers to the reward he received for answering the riddle of the Sphinx: the kingship and Jocasta's hand in marriage. The offspring of this incestuous union are Antigone, Ismene, Eteocles, and Polyneices.

606 / 547 *In the grip of disaster I destroyed and murdered* is the translation of the line as emended by H. Lloyd-Jones in the OCT. The manuscript read-

ing, "I murdered and destroyed others," doesn't make sense in the context, so an emendation is necessary. It is interesting that the text of the play is corrupt in several places where the issue of Oedipus' guilt or innocence is being discussed, clear evidence that this question troubled generations of readers and scribes copying the play.

623 / 562 Theseus was raised in his mother's birthplace, Troezen, without knowledge that his father was Aegeus, king of Athens. Like Oedipus, he learned his true parentage only as an adult.

699 / 632 *our alliance* Theseus seems here to refer to a military alliance that has existed over the generations between the rulers of Athens and the rulers of Thebes. It cannot be an alliance specifically between Oedipus and Theseus, since they did not know each other prior to this meeting.

705 / 637 Here again, a possible corruption in the text has frustrated scholars who wish to determine exactly what kind of legal status Theseus is offering Oedipus. Whether or not Theseus' idea is to incorporate Oedipus fully into Athens as a citizen, it is clear at least that he is offering him a home and the readiness to protect him as if he were a citizen.

732 / 658–60 The OCT here brackets three lines in which Theseus personifies and belittles the threats Oedipus fears. These lines were first deleted by a German scholar in the nineteenth century, and the OCT follows his lead, on aesthetic grounds rather than because of any corruption in the text.

740–75 / 668–719 1st Stasimon: the first of the independent choral songs composed with pairs of stanzas (strophe and antistrophe), each member of the pair having an identical rhythmical pattern.

751 / 683 The *two Great Goddesses* are Demeter and Persephone, mother and daughter, who were the patron goddesses of the Eleusinian Mysteries; these were an extremely popular mystery cult in nearby Eleusis that seems to have offered its initiates a vision of some kind of afterlife, contrary to the commonly held belief that death was the negation of life and the dead were shapeless, empty shadows—nothingness—in the underworld. One of the many beauties of this song to Colonus, Sophocles' birthplace, and by extension to Athens, is its evocation of an eternal city dependent only on this song and the hearts and minds of those who hear it for its existence.

758ff. / 694ff. The last two stanzas celebrate the olive, the bridle, and the oar, evoking Athens' foundation myth, in which Athena and Poseidon give these things to Athens in a competition to become its patron god.

760 / 695 The Doric isle of Pelops is the Peloponnese, the southern mainland of Greece, whose most famous city was Sparta, against which Athens has been waging a war and by which it is about to be defeated (see the Introduction). Sparta was founded by Dorians, whose ethnicity the Athenians considered, seemingly correctly, to be different from their own. The Athenians and Spartans spoke different dialects of Greek that were mutually comprehensible but aurally very distinct.

773ff. / 715ff. The text of the last lines of this ode is corrupt, but the image seems clear. In honoring Poseidon for the gift of the oar that allows man to travel over his realm, the chorus evokes the image of the little waves that the oars make as they dip into the water and sees the "white caps" that also rise on the surface of the sea as the footsteps of the Nereids, nymphs of the sea, accompanying the ship.

776–1149 / 720–1043 2nd Episode: Creon, Oedipus' brother-in-law and uncle, arrives from Thebes to persuade Oedipus to return with him. When Oedipus refuses, Creon tries to force him first by revealing that he has already captured Ismene and then by seizing Antigone. Theseus arrives to stop Creon from dragging Oedipus away also and demands that Creon take him to Antigone and Ismene so that he can restore them to Oedipus. The episode is broken at two points (904–18/833–43, 960–74/876–86) by a strophe and antistrophe in which the chorus, Oedipus, and Creon, we may suppose, sing and mime the action of seizure and resistance.

811 / 757 *purge this shame* The manuscripts preserve here the imperative "hide!" The editors of the OCT mark the verb as corrupt but do not suggest an emendation. The difficulty with the manuscript reading is both that Creon has just said, "I may not hide what is plain to see," so the command to hide seems contradictory, and that there is no object for the verb "hide." However, Creon clearly wants Oedipus to remove himself from the possibility of the world's censure and the shame it brings the family. Hence our "purge this shame."

845–47 / 784–86 Oedipus accuses Creon of pretending that he will allow Oedipus back into Thebes and will eventually allow him to be buried there. Creon's real motive is to keep Oedipus out of Thebes because, as a patricide, he may pollute the city, but ensure that no one else—and particularly not Athens—can receive the protection of his tomb by harboring him and burying him within the boundaries of their city.

893ff. / 826ff. It is exciting to try to imagine how this struggle would have been choreographed in the original production. It is my feeling that, after Antigone is removed bodily from the stage, there is very little physical contact among Creon, Oedipus, and the chorus. Rather, one might imagine a stylized and choreographed struggle between Creon and the chorus that would represent first the chorus's failed attempt to block Antigone's departure and then their successful attempt to keep Creon away from Oedipus. The rhythmic pattern of the lines is excited iambic trimeter, with one character breaking in and completing another's line, alternating with two stanzas of sung lyrics in which Creon, Oedipus, and the chorus snatch the song from each other in short spurts.

968 / 882 The words *Zeus knows* were suggested by the great English editor and commentator on Sophocles, R. Jebb, to fill out a part of this line that had been lost. There are several other suggestions; the OCT offers "Zeus will not bring this about, I know." We prefer Jebb's emendation.

1043 / 947 *your Council—that makes its home on Ares' hill* Creon is referring to the area at the foot of the Acropolis called the Areopagus (Hill of Ares) and the council that met there. One of the oldest governmental institutions to survive into the fourth century, the council changed in both function and membership from its aristrocratic beginnings in the sixth century. Aeschylus' *Oresteia* dramatizes the establishment of the council as a civic replacement for the Furies' role as avengers of crimes against the family, and particularly homicide. This function the council retained throughout its history, but at other times it also was responsible for ensuring that the laws by which the Athenians ruled themselves were upheld.

1050 / 954–55 The OCT follows the editor Blaydes in deleting two of Creon's lines here that seem out of place and inappropriate to Creon's character.

1124–28 / 1028–33 These lines follow, in the manuscript tradition, line 1138 / 1027, where they do not make easy sense. A. E. Housman, whose life and scholarship have recently been dramatized in Tom Stoppard's play *The Invention of Love*, suggested their transposition to the place where the OCT prints them and we have translated them.

1126ff. / 1031ff. Theseus suspects that Creon is being aided in his attempt to remove Oedipus by Athenians who would support Thebes against Athens, if they came into conflict. The remark would resonate strongly with the audience, for whom the issue of Athenian supporters of Sparta against Athenian interests was an immediate reality. It also characterizes Theseus as a careful ruler who is watchful over the good of the whole city, rather than the interest of a faction. In this way, although portrayed as a monarch, Theseus also has a democratic bent to his leadership.

1150–92 / 1044–95 2nd Stasimon: The chorus imagines in its song the struggle over Ismene and Antigone between Theseus and Creon's men. They picture it taking place at some point along the path from Athens to Eleusis, the site of the Eleusinian Mysteries. In this way Theseus' recovery of Ismene and Antigone echoes, however subtly and remotely, Demeter's journey to recover Persephone from the Underworld, which the Eleusinian Mysteries commemorate. The children of Eumolpus are members of the family who, generation after generation, administered the Mysteries as chief priests. The second stanza of this song suggests a different route that the Thebans may have taken that would not bring them to Eleusis.

1193–1334 / 1096–210 3rd Episode: After Theseus returns Antigone and Ismene to Oedipus, he reports the presence of a suppliant at the altar of Poseidon who wishes to speak to Oedipus. Once Oedipus realizes that this is his son/brother Polyneices, he refuses to speak to him, until Antigone persuades him at least to hear what Polyneices has to say.

1242 / 1132 Greeks believed that a man who has committed patricide is polluted and that the stain of his pollution can spread, through contact, to another individual or a community. Exile was a common form of purification and punishment for such pollution, and, in exile, the murderer can commune with others without endangering them. However, the sense Oedipus has here, and that the chorus had earlier, that even in exile he is a danger to those with whom he comes in contact derives from a less formalistic or legalistic sense of his state as a polluted being. Sophocles dramatizes in this moment Oedipus' paradoxical being as both polluted and powerful.

1275 / 1160 To sit upon an altar is to place yourself as a suppliant under the protection of the god and the people within that god's purview. Oedipus therefore knows that the man Theseus is talking about is in need but does not know the nature of the need.

1335–67 / 1211–48 3rd Stasimon: The chorus expresses a pessimistic view of the value of human life in light of the evidence of Oedipus' suffering.

1368–1721 / 1249–555 4th Episode: Polyneices asks Oedipus to join him in his attack on Thebes to depose his brother, Eteocles. Oedipus curses Polyneices and Eteocles, and Polyneices leaves to lead his six allies against Thebes, knowing that the expedition is doomed to failure. Before he leaves he secures from Antigone a promise to bury his body. Between Polyneices' departure and the climactic movement of Oedipus into the grove of the Furies, the chorus sing two pairs of stanzas, 1603–54 / 1447–99, in which they respond to the thunder and lightning that follow Polyneices' departure as omens of some new and strange thing. Between each stanza Oedipus urgently insists that Theseus be summoned, as he knows the thunder and lightning announce his own imminent death. Theseus arrives, and Oedipus rises from his seat unaided and leads Antigone, Ismene, and Theseus into the grove of the Furies.

1389–90 / 1267–68 *But since Compassion shares the throne with Zeus* The word we here translate as Compassion, *Aidos*, appears also at line 260 / 247, where we translate it as *respect*. It also appears as a verb at line 1312–13 / 1192, where we translate it as *show him / some understanding*. *Aidos* is an important concept for understanding the way the Greeks regulated their social behavior. People judged their own behavior by the way they imagined others would view it. *Aidos* could be described as the quality that makes one conscious of, and concerned about, others' opinions of one's behavior. In the first use Antigone is asking the members of chorus, who are in a position to give or to deny Oedipus what he wants, to be aware of how others will judge their treatment of him, if they abuse that power and do not show him respect. At lines 1312–16 / 1192–94, Antigone is appealing to Oedipus to treat Polyneices as other fathers who are angry at their sons do. In this passage Polyneices, who also fears that Oedipus will not give him what he needs, appeals to Oedipus' awareness of how he will be viewed as a father. Antigone, too, has attempted to persuade Oedipus to see Polyneices by warning him of seeming too harsh toward his son.

1436 / 1305 Polyneices describes the alliance of the seven heroes who joined together to attack Thebes under his leadership. The story of the "Seven against Thebes," each hero stationed at one of Thebes' seven gates, was a part of the Oedipus myth that had its own narrative tradition in both epic and drama. Aeschylus' play *The Seven against Thebes* and Euripides' *Suppliants* both treat aspects of this story, for example.

1447 / 1320 Parthenopaeus' name contains the word *parthenos*, which means unmarried girl, virgin. Atalanta, Parthenopaeus' mother, resisted marriage by insisting that only a man who could beat her in a foot race could marry her. She killed those she could overtake. She was finally defeated by Melanion, who distracted her in the race with golden apples given to him by Aphrodite. Their son was Parthenopaeus.

1519 / 1375 Presumably, Oedipus here refers to curses he made against his sons when he was first exiled.

1558 / 1410 Polyneices' request of Antigone to bury his body when he dies at Thebes had provided Sophocles, thirty-five years earlier, with the subject for his *Antigone*. His reference to the events of that play here reminds the audience that Oedipus' curse on his sons is the indirect cause of his beloved Antigone's death. Thus Oedipus, despite his great power, is also seen to be subject to a rhythm of events outside his control.

1577 / 1426 Polyneices' inability to act in defiance of Oedipus' curse is the flip side of his refusal to respond to Oedipus' desire when he was being exiled. Both the refusal and the submission characterize Polyneices as a figure who is unable successfully to establish his own independence in the face of the controlling forces of his life.

1586 / 1434 *my father and his Furies* This phrase is ambiguous, and our understanding of Polyneices differs considerably depending on what we think he means here. By the reference to Oedipus' Furies, Polyneices may be blaming Oedipus' own terrible past for Polyneices' own terrible future, or he may refer to Oedipus' curse as his Furies—the punishment he has been able to evoke for Polyneices' treatment of him.

1623 / 1468 *What end will he unleash upon us?* is a translation of the text as transmitted by the manuscripts, understanding Zeus, or possibly Oedipus, as the subject. Alternatively, one could understand the lightning as the subject ("What end will it unleash upon us?"), but then the objection of the editors of the OCT that it is hard to understand how lightning might produce an "end" seems valid. The editors of the OCT emend the text to read "Truly, he will release his weapon." We have chosen to keep the manuscript reading and understand Zeus as the subject. Zeus' sending of the lightning can be seen as the sign of the end to which he is bringing Oedipus.

1678–81 / 1522–25 The place where Oedipus dies becomes the site of a hero cult that was still a place of worship in Sophocles' time.

1693 / 1534 The dragon-seed men are the Thebans, whose ancestors sprang from dragon's teeth sowed in the earth by Cadmus.

1703 / 1542 This spectacular moment, when Oedipus rises and leads the others through the central door of the skene unaided, corresponds dramatically to the scene at the beginning of the play when Antigone helps Oedipus move with great difficulty from the grove to the rock where he has been sitting throughout the play, until this moment. The transformation of Oedipus that is implied in the contrast between these two moments lies at the center of the play's mystery (see the Introduction, pp. 5–8, for further discussion).

1712 / 1548 The *guide Hermes* is a reference to the god Hermes' function as the psychopomp, the leader of the dead down into the underworld; the goddess "who dwells beneath" is Persephone, Demeter's and Zeus' daughter and wife of Hades.

1722–40 / 1556–78 4th Stasimon: The song that the chrous sings, wishing for an easy death for Oedipus, makes reference to the gods of the dead, Persephone (the "unseen Goddess") and Hades ("the master of those who dwell in darkness, Aidoneus"). Aidoneus is another name for the god of the dead. The "goddesses of earth" are the Eumenides, and the "invincible creature" asleep at the entrance of Hades is the three-headed dog Cerberus, whose presence at the entrance to the underworld keeps the living from descending and the dead from ascending.

1741–977 / 1579–779 Exodos: A messenger describes the ritual preparation of Oedipus for his death, his farewell to his daughters, the voice of a god summoning him, and his final mysterious disappearance that only Theseus witnesses. The Messenger speech is a rich dramatic device frequently used by Sophocles and Euripides. It allows the playwright to narrate action that would be impossible to represent on stage. Both Sophocles and Euripides incorporate detailed visual information into these speeches in order to let the audience "see" what has happened offstage. In this case Sophocles has included very precise geographical markers that would, we suppose, evoke a landscape known in reality to the audience. Of course, none of the details of the landscape has survived, so that we cannot know how close to reality Sophocles has made this description.

1853–949 / 1670–750 The final *kommos* of the play takes the form of a lament for the dead. Antigone and Ismene as the surviving female members of the family would, under normal circumstances, perform a ritual lament at the tomb of their father. Here, since they cannot approach the place of Oedipus' death, their song must have given the audience a powerful sense of unanchored dislocation. Antigone echoes this sense of dislocation when she asks first to be taken to Oedipus' tomb and then to be allowed to go home to Thebes. The lack of spatial focus at the end of the play is an important coda to the intense certainty of Oedipus' movement toward and knowledge of his death place and leaves the audience with a sense of disorienting uncertainty. The meter of the *kommos* incorporates a fair number of iambic lines that we have printed as part of the sung lyrics, although it is possible that these lines were spoken or chanted rather than sung.

1869 / (1681) *Invisible Fields* is a reference to the underworld, where all things lose form and substance.

1950–77 / 1751–79 The final lines of the play, a conversation between Theseus and Antigone in anapaestic rhythm, start the action narrated in Sophocles' play *Antigone*, as Theseus promises to secure Antigone's return to Thebes, where she hopes to stop her brothers' civil war. This final ironic twist, after Theseus' promise to Oedipus to protect Antigone and Ismene, returns the audience, after the mystery of Oedipus' death, to the tension between power and powerlessness that Oedipus—and all mankind—never escapes.

1964–65 / 1766–77 *And the god / heard us* Sophocles does not specify which god is meant here, just as it is unclear which god speaks to Oedipus just before he dies. In both cases he seems to evoke a nameless divine power attending the end of Oedipus' life to deepen the mystery of that end. That Oath, too, is present marks the paramount importance of the binding pact between Theseus and Oedipus that ensures Athens a future "free of suffering," the form of which is also shrouded in mystery.

GLOSSARY

ADRASTOS: The king of Argos whose daughter Polyneices marries in order to make a military alliance with Argos against Thebes.

AIDONEUS: Another name for Hades, god of the dead.

ANTIGONE: Daughter of Oedipus and Jocasta; sister of Oedipus, Ismene, Polyneices, and Eteocles.

APHRODITE: Goddess of desire.

APOLLO: also called Phoebus. Apollo's oracle at Delphi has delivered a number of prophesies to Oedipus over the course of his life.

ARES: God of war.

ARGOS: An ancient city in the Peloponnese, important both in the mythic tradition and as a power with wavering allegiances in the Peloponnesian War.

ARTEMIS: Sister of Apollo, goddess of the hunt and wild animals.

ATALANTA: A mythic figure who resisted marriage by challenging all her suitors to a foot race. When she was beaten by Hippomenes (a.k.a. Melanion, Hippomedon), she married him and gave birth to Parthenopaeus, one of the six leaders who join Polyneices in his attack on Thebes.

ATHENA: Daughter of Zeus, also called Pallas, a patron goddess of Athens.

CADMUS: The founder of Thebes; Thebans are sometimes called Cadmeians or dragon-seed men, because of the story that Cadmus created the first inhabitants of his city by sowing the teeth of the dragon he had slain in the earth.

CEPHISUS: River in Attica that was said rarely to run dry, as most rivers did and do in the hot summer months.

DEMETER: Goddess of fertility and grain who, with her daughter Persephone, was worshipped at Eleusis.

DIONYSOS: God of wine, ecstatic possession, and illusion. Dionysos' festival in Athens was the occasion for the performance of many of the plays we know as Greek tragedy. Also had a role in the Eleusinian Mysteries and in the sanctuary at Delphi.

ELEUSIS: Site of the Eleusinian Myseries, a mystery cult that was widely popular at the time of the *Oedipus at Colonus*. These mysteries are believed to offer to initiates some vision of an afterlife.

ETEOCLES: Brother of Antigone, Ismene, Polyneices, and Oedipus. Though the younger son, he claims the throne of Thebes from his older brother Polyneices.

EUMENIDES: Also called Furies, Erinyes, or the Dread Goddesses. Ancient earth goddesses who avenge crimes by family members against their families.

EUMOLPUS: Founder of the family who provided the high priests for the Eleusinian Mysteries.

FURIES: See Eumenides.

HADES: Brother of Zeus and Poseidon, husband of Persephone, god of the dead.

HELIOS: God of the sun.

HERMES : God who guides the shades of the dead to the underworld.

JOCASTA: Mother and wife of Oedipus, wife of Laius, sister of Creon. When she learns she has married her son, she hangs herself.

LABDACUS: Father of Laius.

LAIUS: Father of Oedipus; killed by Oedipus at a crossroads among Delphi, Thebes, and Corinth.

NEREIDS: Nymphs of the sea.

PERITHOUS: Companion of Theseus in some of his exploits, including a descent to the underworld.

PERSEPHONE: Daughter of Demeter, wife of Hades, goddess of the underworld.

PHOEBUS: Another name for Apollo.

POLYNEICES: Brother of Antigone, Ismene, Eteocles, and Oedipus. Polyneices is driven into exile by Eteocles and forms an alliance with the king of Argos to attack Thebes and take back his throne.

POSEIDON: Brother of Zeus and Hades, god of the sea. A patron god of Athens.

RHEA: Ancient earth goddess, mother of Zeus, Poseidon, Hades, and Ares.

STYX: The river that runs through the underworld.

TARTARUS: The underworld.

THESEUS: The legendary king of Athens, son of Aegeus, and slayer of the Minotaur in the labyrinth in Crete.

FURTHER READING

GENERAL

Arnott, P. *Public and Performance in the Greek Theatre*. London, 1989.

Easterling, P. E., ed. *The Cambridge Companion to Greek Tragedy*. Cambridge, Eng., 1997.

Wiles, D. *Greek Theatre Performance: An Introduction*. Cambridge, Eng., 2000.

Winkler, J. J., and F. I. Zeitlin, eds. *Nothing to Do with Dionysos? Athenian Drama in Its Social Context*. Princeton, 1990.

SOPHOCLES

Reinhardt, K. *Sophocles*. Trans. by H. and D. Harvey. Oxford, 1979.

Segal, C. *Sophocles' Tragic World: Divinity, Nature, Society*. Cambridge, Mass., and London, 1995.

Taplin, O. "Lyric Dialogue and Dramatic Construction in Later Sophocles." *Dioniso* 55 (1985): 115–22.

Winnington-Ingram, R. P. *Sophocles: An Interpretation*. Cambridge, Eng., 1980.

OEDIPUS AT COLONUS

Birge, D. "The Grove of the Eumenides: Refuge and Hero Shrine in *Oedipus at Colonus*." *Classical Journal* 80 (1984): 1–17.

Burian, P. "Suppliant and Saviour: Oedipus at Colonus." *Phoenix* 28 (1974): 408–29.

Edmunds, L. *Theatrical Space and Historical Place in Sophocles' Oedipus at Colonus*. Lanham, Md., and London, 1996.

Slatkin, L. "Oedipus at Colonus: Exile and Integration." In P. Euben, ed., *Greek Tragedy and Political Theory* (Berkeley, 1986).

RELIGION AND MYTH

Edmunds, L. *Oedipus: The Ancient Legend and Its Later Analogues*. Baltimore and London, 1985.

Farnell, L. R. *Greek Hero Cults and Ideas of Immortality*. Oxford, 1896–1909.

Gould, J. "Hiketeia." *Journal of Hellenic Studies* 93 (1973): 74–103.

Mylonas, G. *Eleusis and the Eleusinian Mysteries*. Princeton, 1961.

Parker, R. C. T. *Miasma: Pollution and Purification in Early Greek Religion*. Oxford, 1983.